WOMEN'S TENNIS TACTICS

WOMEN'S TENNIS TACTICS

Rob Antoun

HUMAN KINETICS

Library of Congress Cataloging-in-Publication Data

Antoun, Rob, 1968-
  Women's tennis tactics / Rob Antoun.
    p. cm.
  Includes bibliographical references and index.
  ISBN-13: 978-0-7360-6572-6 (soft cover)
  ISBN-10: 0-7360-6572-5 (soft cover)
  1. Tennis--Training. 2. Tennis--Singles. 3. Tennis--Doubles. 4. Women tennis players. I. Title.
  GV1002.9.T7A58 2007
  796.342082--dc22

                    2006039394

ISBN-10: 0-7360-6572-5
ISBN-13: 978-0-7360-6572-6

Description of 'touch and feel' on page 93 reprinted, by permission, from P. Roetert and J. Groppel, 2001, *World-class tennis technique* (Champaign, IL: Human Kinetics), 233.

Acquisitions Editor: Laurel Plotzke; **Developmental Editor:** Amanda Eastin; **Assistant Editor:** Christine Horger; **Copyeditor:** Patsy Fortney; **Proofreader:** Jim Burns; **Indexer:** Craig Brown; **Permission Manager:** Carly Breeding; **Graphic Designer:** Bob Reuther; **Graphic Artist:** Francine Hamerski; **Photo Manager:** Laura Fitch; **Cover Designer:** Keith Blomberg; **Photographer (cover):** Lisa Blumenfeld/Getty Images; **Art Manager:** Kelly Hendren; **Illustrator:** Tammy Page; **Printer:** Versa Press

Human Kinetics books are available at special discounts for bulk purchase. Special editions or book excerpts can also be created to specification. For details, contact the Special Sales Manager at Human Kinetics.

Printed in the United States of America   10 9 8 7 6 5 4 3 2 1

Human Kinetics
Web site: www.HumanKinetics.com

United States: Human Kinetics, P.O. Box 5076, Champaign, IL 61825-5076
800-747-4457
e-mail: humank@hkusa.com

Canada: Human Kinetics, 475 Devonshire Road Unit 100, Windsor, ON N8Y 2L5
800-465-7301 (in Canada only)
e-mail: orders@hkcanada.com

Europe: Human Kinetics, 107 Bradford Road, Stanningley, Leeds LS28 6AT, United Kingdom
+44 (0) 113 255 5665
e-mail: hk@hkeurope.com

Australia: Human Kinetics, 57A Price Avenue, Lower Mitcham, South Australia 5062
08 8372 0999
e-mail: liaw@hkaustralia.com

New Zealand: Human Kinetics, Division of Sports Distributors NZ Ltd., P.O. Box 300 226 Albany, North Shore City, Auckland
0064 9 448 1207
e-mail: info@humankinetics.co.nz

To my wife Catherine and son Jake. Without your love and support this wouldn't have been possible. To my first coach Derrick Haines for helping me fall in love with the game, and to Charles Bailey, Bill Knight, and Keith Sohl for giving me such great coaching opportunities.

CONTENTS

Drill Finder viii

Key to Diagrams. x

Preface xi

Acknowledgments. xiii

Introduction xv

1 Tactical Serving. 1

The Dominating First Serve 2

The Effective Second Serve 16

Serving Percentages 24

2 Tactical Returning 43

The Neutralising First Serve Return. 45

The Aggressive Second Serve Return 56

Returning Percentages 68

3 Playing the Baseline 83

Building From the Baseline 84

Attacking From the Baseline 93

Defending From the Baseline 97

Assessing Baseline Play 101

4 Playing the Net. **131**

Instinctual Net Play 133

Planned Net Play. 135

Standing Ground at the Net. 143

Using Anticipation at the Net. 144

5 Opposing the Net Player **161**

Two-Ball Pass 162

Lob 163

Defending With the Double Bluff 165

Assessing Net Play 167

6 Developing a Game Style. **175**

Stages of Tactical Development 176

Developing Winning Patterns of Play 184

Personal Factors 185

Glossary **197**

References **203**

Index. **205**

About the Author. **211**

DRILL FINDER

First Serve Drills

Drill 1.1   Hitting the Attacking Forehand After a First Serve 28
Drill 1.2   Dominating With the First Serve..29
Drill 1.3   Holding Serve Even When the Opponent Knows the Tactic 30
Drill 1.4   Using Only Three First Serves per Game 31
Drill 1.5   Using the First Serve to Create an Advantage 32
Drill 1.6   Maintaining Control After the First Serve......................................33
Drill 1.7   Using the Drive Volley After the First Serve 34
Drill 1.8   Using the Sneak After the First Serve 35
Drill 1.9   Practicing the Serve and Volley Tactic..36

Second Serve Drills

Drill 1.11   Developing Accuracy of the Second Serve 37
Drill 1.12   Constructing a Second Serve Pattern by Visualising
             the Returner's Court Position 38
Drill 1.13   Neutralising the Point Using a Second Serve Pattern 39
Drill 1.14   Disguising the Direction of the Second Serve 40
Drill 1.15   Serving With Accuracy and Variety of Direction 40
Drill 1.16   Moving the Returner Out of Position to Maintain Second
             Serve Dominance 41
Drill 1.17   Improving Variety of Spin, Direction, and Power When Serving 42

First Serve Return Drills

Drill 2.1   Developing the Middle Return 72
Drill 2.2   Neutralising With the Inside-Out Return.......................................73
Drill 2.3   Using the Inside-In Return to Move the Server 74
Drill 2.4   Using the Blocked Return to Turn Defence Into Attack 75

Second Serve Return Drills

Drill 2.5   Returning From an Aggressive Court Position 76
Drill 2.6   Dominating With the Second Serve Return...................................77
Drill 2.7   Maintaining Baseline Control After the Return 78
Drill 2.8   Using the Drive Volley After the Return 79
Drill 2.9   Using the Sneak After the Return...80
Drill 2.10   Using the Return and Planned Approach......................................81

Baseline Accuracy and Consistency Drills

Drill 3.1   Counting the Quality Shots... 107
Drill 3.2   Scoring Only With Unforced Errors 108
Drill 3.4   Changing the Direction of the Ball From the Baseline 110
Drill 3.6   Baseline Construction 112
Drill 3.7   Counting the Target Hits 114

Early Court Position and Movement Drills

Drill 3.3   Playing to a Higher Tempo From the Baseline 109
Drill 3.5   Running Drives From the Baseline 111
Drill 3.14   Improving Movement Around the Baseline 121
Drill 3.15   Hitting at the Top of the Bounce 122
Drill 3.16   Encouraging an Aggressive Court Position 122
Drill 3.17   Finishing the Point With the Shoulder-High Attack 123

Drills to Develop Variety

Drill 3.8   Avoiding the Diamond 116
Drill 3.9   The Forbidden Square 117
Drill 3.10   Developing the Aggressive Loop 118
Drill 3.11   Playing With 'Space, Not Pace' 119
Drill 3.12   Disguising the Drop Shot 119

Defending Drills

Drill 3.18   Developing the Counterpunch Tactic 124
Drill 3.19   Defending With Depth 125
Drill 3.20   Defending Against the Switch Shot 126
Drill 3.21   Using the Two-Ball Defence 127
Drill 3.23   Defending Against the Drop Shot 129

Approach and Net Play Drills

Drill 4.1   Using the Drive Volley to Attack 148
Drill 4.2   Developing the Sneak Volley 149
Drill 4.3   Developing a Planned Approach Shot 150
Drill 4.4   Developing the Short Angle and Deep-Down-the-Line Volley 151
Drill 4.5   Developing Power and Direction of the Smash 152
Drill 4.6   Winning With the Smash 153
Drill 4.7   Combining the Volley and Smash 154
Drill 4.8   Playing the Volley and Smash With Consistency 155
Drill 4.11   Standing Ground When Under Pressure at the Net 158

Passing Shot and Lob Drills

Drill 5.1   Using the Two-Ball Pass Tactic 170
Drill 5.2   Using the Aggressive and Defensive Lob 171
Drill 5.3   Improving the Running Passing Shot and Lob 172
Drill 5.4   Defending With the Double Bluff 173

Perception and Anticipation Drills

Drill 3.13   Developing Perception Skills 120
Drill 4.13   Developing Tactical and Technical Anticipation 160

Doubles Drills

Drill 1.10   Dominating the Net as a Serving Team 37
Drill 2.11   Developing the Return and Planned Approach in Doubles 82
Drill 3.22   Defending as a Team in Doubles 128
Drill 4.9   Using the Intercept Volley in Doubles 156
Drill 4.10   Working as a Doubles Team at the Net 157
Drill 4.12   Defending the Net as a Doubles Team 159
Drill 5.5   Playing Against a Doubles Team at the Net 174

KEY TO DIAGRAMS

S	Server
SP	Server's partner
R	Returner
RP	Returner's partner
P	Player
O	Opponent
F	Feeder
CO	Coach
T	Target

———▶   Path of player

– – –▶   Path of ball

PREFACE

This book is one of the most comprehensive guides to women's tennis ever written. It is unique because it is the first to separate the tactics used in the women's game from those used in the men's game. There are significant differences between the two sexes in the way the game is played today, and the specific requirements for female tennis players now need to be studied in their own right. *Women's Tennis Tactics* does exactly this.

Women's Tennis Tactics will help players, coaches, and parents who are involved in women's tennis at all levels. It provides fascinating insight into the various tactics that are used by today's top players, offers tactical solutions to the challenges that all players face during matches, and will help the aspiring player to develop a game style based on her own specific strengths. It also includes numerous coaching tips and drills that can be used to improve the understanding and execution of each tactic.

Each of the five game situations in tennis is studied in a separate chapter (serving, returning, playing from the baseline, approaching and playing at the net, and opposing the net player). The most commonly used tactics within each of these game situations are discussed, both in singles and doubles, and a relevant practice drill is recommended with each one. Discussion of doubles play is indicated in the text by the double-racket icon. Each chapter also includes suggestions for how to record tactical information to help a player develop her game for the future.

Chapter 1 studies the tactical options for a player when serving. It discusses the key differences between the first and second serve and how these affect a player's ability to control the game. Crucially, it shows how a player can use an effective serve in a number of winning patterns of play and how she can improve a weaker one and use it to neutralise the potential threat of an opponent.

The return of serve is arguably the most important shot in women's tennis today, and chapter 2 devotes time to helping a player use this shot to great advantage. Again, the varying tactical options between the first and second serve return are analysed, along with the returner's choice of second shot with each. The differences between facing a right- and left-handed server are also considered in addition to the key physical and mental skills that are required to return effectively.

Chapter 3 helps a player build an advantage from the baseline, use her best attacking shot to finish the point with, and defend effectively when under pressure. This is done by improving her consistency, accuracy, and variety of shot when playing from the back, as well as developing the best possible court position and a proactive, problem-solving mentality.

The ways female players are approaching and playing at the net have changed in recent years; these methods are discussed in detail in chapter 4. Crucially, a player will learn how to use the instinctual approach, as well as the more traditional planned approach, when attacking the net. This chapter highlights the various shots players can use with these two tactics, along with the anticipatory skills that are required. It also addresses the volley and smash options available to a player once she is at the net.

Chapter 5 considers the choices a player faces when her opponent plays at the net. Knowing when and where to hit the passing shot is vital, as well as understanding when best to use the aggressive and defensive lob. Helping a player make these tactical decisions is central to this chapter, along with discussing the movement required to play these shots most effectively.

Chapter 6 helps a player build her own game style by progressing through the four key stages of tactical development. This includes highlighting specific patterns of play, as well as making smart tactical decisions and problem-solving effectively. This chapter also suggests ways for coaches and parents to 'hand over' more responsibility to a player when the time is right. All of these factors will help a player improve her game significantly.

Women's Tennis Tactics is a comprehensive resource that can be used by anyone involved in the women's game. It will help the promising junior as much as the seasoned pro, and it offers coaches and parents the insight they need to help their players succeed on their tennis journeys.

ACKNOWLEDGMENTS

There are numerous friends, colleagues, and players whom I would like to thank for their support and encouragement of this project over the last five years: Mike Barrell, Cara Black, Claire Curran, Eric Dochtermann, Paul Fisher, Mandy Franks, Dan George, Jason Goodall, Clint Harris, Iain Hughes, Amy Jensen, Ann Jones, Brent Larkham, Carl Maes, Steven Martens, Craig Morris, Jonathan Munday, Erwan Nicolas, James Rose, Nigel Sears, Asa Svensson, Elena Tatarkova, Daniel Thorp, and Nick Weal.

I would also like to thank Jan Felgate and Penny Mulliner at IMG; Abigail Tordoff at Octagon; Meg Stavrakopoulou at IBM; and Mandy Eastin, Laurel Plotzke, and Penny Clarke at Human Kinetics.

In particular, I would like to thank Alistair Higham for his invaluable support at every stage of this book and Paul Dent for his creative and challenging ideas that have helped me throughout my career.

Thanks to all the players that I have had the privilege to work with, especially Hannah Collin, whose tennis journey allowed me to learn at the highest level.

Finally, thanks to Mum and Dad and the rest of my family for always being there.

INTRODUCTION

As the female game continues to evolve, the differences between it and the male game appear more marked.

    —Steven Martens (2006 Davis Cup Captain, Belgium) and Carl Maes (2006 Federation Cup Captain, Belgium)

Women's tennis has enjoyed a huge increase in popularity worldwide in recent years. As with most other sports, it has benefitted from major improvements in coaching methods, training techniques, and equipment. As a result, female players are becoming faster and stronger and are playing the game at a higher tempo than ever before. Today's top players are now widely admired for their strength, athleticism, and determination, and have become valuable role models for the next generation of athletes. Female players also appear to be playing the game very differently from male players, and these differences are becoming greater as time goes on.

The significant physical discrepancies between men and women have a huge bearing on how and why the game is played so differently. Generally, women are shorter and lighter, hold less muscle mass than men do, and possess significantly less upper- and lower-body strength also. Specifically, females have 54 percent of male upper-body strength and 68 percent of male lower-body strength (Pluim 1999). This contrast in strength means that female players tend to play from different court positions using different techniques than their male counterparts.

To hit the ball hard, the female player will tend to play farther up the court (i.e., closer to, or from inside, the baseline). Hitting the ball early allows her to use the speed of the oncoming ball to create time and pace pressure on her opponent. She will tend to hit the ball with less spin as a result of this because, to play from inside the baseline, her technique needs to be as efficient as possible. This means hitting the ball with short, simple swings that are easy to coordinate and that produce less spin. Indeed, this is a big reason the double-handed backhand is such a popular shot in women's tennis. This shot allows the player to absorb the pace of the oncoming ball more easily because the two hands provide extra strength. It is also easy to coordinate because the swing is shorter as a result.

By contrast, male players often choose to play from farther behind the baseline. The extra body strength that they possess, compared to women, allows them to impart heavier spin on the ball (by using stronger arm and shoulder units) from deeper positions behind the baseline, enabling them to use more of the court and its surroundings. It also allows them to use the forehand more as a weapon. The single-handed forehand uses a longer swing and involves more body parts in its execution than the backhand does. In other words, it has a longer coordination chain that requires more complex coordination and strength to hit effectively. However, the single-handed forehand generally allows the player to hit the ball much harder than he could with the backhand, and it creates more spin and angle from a wider range of court positions.

Male players also play with a stronger reliance on the serve (they win a higher percentage of first and second serve points), compared to women, who rely more heavily on the return of serve (because there are usually more breaks of serve in a women's match). Again, the greater physical strength of the male player allows him to create more serving power, as well as topspin, to dominate an opponent. This combination simply enables him to hold serve more often. Female players, on the other hand, will prefer to create slice on the serve because less strength is needed to control and move the ball in an aggressive manner. The slice serve moves in an opposite direction to the topspin serve, thereby creating different tactical patterns for the female player to build on.

Furthermore, women tend to approach and play from the net less frequently than men do. They choose their moments to approach more carefully (using more 'instinctual' approaches than planned approaches) and, not surprisingly, enjoy a higher success rate when doing so. This is because they tend to use the volley as a 'finish' shot, with much of the work in creating an advantage done from the baseline before the volley is played. Male players, on the other hand, tend to approach the net more often—using a combination of planned and instinctual approaches—and are prepared to take more risks in the process.

The ability of the male player to use more of the court and its surroundings and to hit a wider selection of shots means that the men's game tends to have more tactical variety. Female players are tending to play with less variation, with a few exceptions, because they are hitting the ball earlier and flatter, with the intention of dominating their opponent as soon as possible in the rally.

These differences become even more apparent when the tennis season switches court surfaces. In the men's game, certain players strongly favour a particular court surface over another because their game style is well suited to it. Male players tend to show stronger preferences because of the more diverse range of shots that they use. The clay court season, for example, often allows a different group of players to excel, compared to the grass court season. In fact, between 1995 and 2005, only two male French Open champions won Grand Slam titles on other surfaces (Andre Agassi and Yevgeny Kafelnikov), compared to six female champions (Steffi Graf, Arantxa Sanchez-Vicario, Mary Pierce, Jennifer Capriati, Serena Williams, and Justine Henin-Hardenne). In the women's game, therefore, far fewer 'specialists' excel on only one surface. The majority of top female players impose their game style on the court surface, as well as their opponent, without needing to make big changes to the way they play.

The fact that females physically mature earlier than males do also affects their tactical development, because this means that a young player can start competing with her more senior counterparts far earlier. At 14 years of age, for example, a girl can compete far more effectively in the senior game than a boy of a similar age can. Indeed, it is not uncommon to see a girl of this age start to compete at a professional level—something rarely, if ever, seen in the men's game. This is because the physical differences between a girl and a woman are smaller than those between a boy and a man at this stage. As a result, the 'development window' for girls stays open for less time (or at least it closes earlier) than it does for boys. In other words, girls have fewer opportunities to develop a variety of tactics because of the expectation to compete at a senior level at a much earlier age. This is important because research suggests that players have less chance of developing their game once competition becomes the main priority. Boys, therefore, have more time to develop and experiment with their game because competing at a senior level remains only a distant ambition during their early teenage years.

As a female player matures and gains experience, she will begin to develop her game style. A player's game style simply represents how she plays the game of tennis. It is made up of a number of factors, including her technical ability, physical condition, mental strength, and tactical intelligence. (How these performance factors shape a player's game style is discussed in detail in chapter 6.)

There are three traditional game styles in women's tennis: baseline, all-court, and serve and volley—all of which have been exhibited by great champions of the past. The baseline player plays the majority of her tennis from the baseline, using powerful and accurate groundstrokes to win points. These groundstrokes are the bedrock of her game. This game style characterised players such as Chris Evert, Tracy Austin, Arantxa Sanchez-Vicario, and Monica Seles, who were four of the most consistent, accurate, and resilient baseline players of all time. The all-court player is comfortable playing from all areas of the court and finishes her points at the net far more often than the baseline player does. She plays with more tactical variety because she uses a wider range of shots, and she is capable of adjusting her tactics quickly if necessary. Perhaps Billie Jean King epitomised this style of play best of all, with players such as Gabriella Sabatini and Steffi Graf also experiencing huge success by using an all-court game in addition to strong baseline play. The serve and volley player is most comfortable playing from the net. She often uses her serve *and* her return to approach the net with, and she relies heavily on good volley and smash technique. Martina Navratilova dominated her opponents for many years using this game style.

From a tactical viewpoint today, many women are learning how to dictate the point at the earliest opportunity, and the majority of their tactics now reflect this common theme. Such aggressive tactical intent has meant that the game styles of many top players now look very similar. Indeed, it seems that the three traditional game styles in women's tennis are continually moving closer together as the game evolves. The baseline player is hitting the ball earlier and with such power and precision that she is naturally finishing points at the net more often. The all-court player is playing with much more aggression from the back of the court and differs from the baseline player only in the number of approaches she makes to the net. The serve and volley player now has to play more aggressively, and more often, from the baseline also. She has to choose her moments to serve and volley more carefully because the return and passing shot have improved so much. These recent trends have left the two extreme ends of tactical variety almost extinct. The all-out serve and volley player and the defensive baseline player now struggle to find a niche in the modern game. The serve and volley tactic is being used more selectively (although it is still effective when used at the right times), and very few players on the WTA Tour rely solely on consistency, without dominance, from the back of the court.

Players such as Lindsay Davenport, Serena and Venus Williams, Jennifer Capriati, Kim Clijsters, and Maria Sharapova are recent examples of the modern-day power player who looks to assert her game against anyone, on any surface. These players have helped take women's tennis to a new level in recent years and have forged the way for a new breed of aggressive, all-court power player in the future. Their tactics have been based around dominating with the serve and return, as well as hitting hard, flat groundstrokes from on, or inside, the baseline whenever possible. Without a doubt, the next generation of players will continue to use the same tactics to an even greater extent.

Some players are exceptions to this rule, however, and they often find that their success lies in the fact that they offer a different style of play from the majority—even though the intention of dominating their opponent remains the same. Recently, players such as Justine Henin-Hardenne and Amelie Mauresmo have experienced great success by playing with more variety of shot—particularly on their single-handed backhand side. The fact that they can hit aggressively with slice and topspin, as well as absorb the pace of the oncoming ball, has proved to be an extremely useful asset for both players.

Henin-Hardenne—with her ability to hit topspin serves, create sharp angles from both forehand and backhand groundstrokes, and play confidently from the net—is a fine example of how variety can be used to dictate an opponent. Martina Hingis, on the other hand, has experienced great success by using variety in a slightly different way. Hingis developed into a highly intelligent counterpuncher by absorbing the pace of her opponent's shot and sending the ball back with a high degree of accuracy and consistency. She used efficient technique and quick, balanced movement, combined with acute tactical awareness, to frustrate and pressure her rivals for many years. She continues to do so today after taking a break from the game. This type of counterpunching player is occasionally seen on the women's tour (Martina Hingis and Anastasia Myskina, for example), as is the player who uses variety as a weapon. Nevertheless, both of these game styles remain in the minority, compared to that of the more powerful, aggressive baseline player.

No matter what game style they use, however, the one common theme among all top players is that they are tactically astute. Every successful player knows what she is good at, knows how she wants to play, and uses tactics within her game style to maximum effect. For example, a baseline player (her game style) may try to attack with her backhand after hitting her first serve—by using the serve and groundstroke attack tactic. An all-court player (her game style) may try to play from the net whenever her opponent is under pressure—by using the sneak approach tactic. In other words, a player will use tactics that incorporate her best shots as often as possible.

Very often these shots will be hit in recognised sequences—called patterns of play—and are repeated throughout a match, season, and even career. For example, the baseline player using the serve and groundstroke attack tactic may use the specific pattern of serving out wide from the deuce court before hitting her backhand crosscourt into the space. The all-court player using the sneak approach tactic will use the pattern of hitting the short angle slice backhand that pulls her opponent short and wide of the court. Patterns of play, therefore, are the specific sequences of shots that players use to execute their favourite tactics.

> If you watch closely, you see professional players use certain repetitive patterns of play over and over again. They have developed certain combinations of shots from years of practice, and they rely on those patterns when they compete.
> —Ron Woods and Mary Joe Fernandez, quoted in *World-Class Tennis Technique* by Paul Roetert and Jack Groppel, Human Kinetics

Being tactically astute also means being aware of an opponent's strengths and weaknesses, as well as being able to use good perception and anticipation skills to sense attacking and defending opportunities ahead of time. These skills simply allow a player to make smart tactical decisions. In other words, being able to read the game *and* the opponent allows a player to choose the most relevant tactics and patterns for every competitive situation.

This book examines the most common tactics seen in the modern game and provides examples of the best patterns of play to use with each one. This is done through a range of practical drills and coaching tips tailored for all levels of play from the beginner to the pro. Some drills are aimed at a specific level (i.e., beginner, intermediate, or advanced), whereas others are relevant for all players. In the context of this book, the term *intermediate* applies to a junior or senior player who is starting tournament play and is close to playing team matches at club level. The *advanced* player will range from experienced club or regional standard through to the professional ranks. Many of the drills encourage a player to observe and assess both her own play and that of her opponent. The skill of analysing an opponent is crucial (and is often underpracticed), yet doing this allows a player to capitalise on an opponent's relevant strengths and weaknesses and helps her to develop a better 'reading' of the game in general.

The tactical side of the game is studied in detail from all five playing situations (i.e., serving, returning, playing from the baseline, approaching and playing at the net, and opposing the net player) in both singles and doubles. A player's tactical development is charted in chapter 6, in which the four key stages of development are considered for junior and senior players alike, along with how personal factors such as decision making, problem solving, and responsibility shape a player's game style. This book explains how each shot, when executed well and at the right time, can be used to gain maximum tactical advantage. Developing tactical awareness in this way is crucial to a player's success—and should be at the heart of every tennis programme.

1

Tactical Serving

© Getty Images

In women's tennis the need to serve more effectively has become greater in recent years because the game is being played more aggressively, and rallies are becoming shorter as a result. How well a female player starts each point is now vital. A strong serve will often create an immediate opportunity for her to dominate, whereas a weaker one gives her opponent the chance to dictate the rally instead. Without a doubt, the tactical momentum in each point will often be determined by the quality of the serve.

The serve is also the one shot in the game that a player has total control over, as well as being the easiest to practice. However, many players simply do not practice their serve often enough. What they don't realise is that regular serving practice can make a huge difference to their game. Like the top golfer who routinely hits hundreds of balls on the practice range to fine-tune technique and maintain a rhythmical swing, the tennis player should practice her serve.

Consistent serving practice is essential for building the power, accuracy, and variety required to carry out the most popular serving tactics in women's tennis today. Furthermore, when studying serving tactics, players should regard the serve as part of an overall strategy. This means looking not only at how and where to serve but also at what to do with the shots that follow it. Therefore, many of the tactics discussed in this chapter include the serve as part of a combination of shots. Consideration is also given to the server's movement and court positioning after serving.

This chapter analyses all of the key serving tactics and gives examples of the various patterns of play that can be used with each one. These include tactics for the baseliner, all-court player, and serve and volleyer, as well as for the aspiring doubles team. First serve tactics are discussed separately from second serve tactics because the first serve is used more often as a weapon. Players tend to hit this shot with more 'adventure' because they know they have another attempt if they miss. The second serve, on the other hand, is hit more safely because it must go in! However, a player with an exceptionally strong second serve could naturally use first serve tactics for both serves.

The Dominating First Serve

Now, more than at any other time in the history of the women's game, the first serve is being used as a weapon. Not only has its power increased—average serving speeds among Wimbledon's top 10 fastest female servers rose from 165.1 km/h (103.2 mph) in 1992 to 189.6 km/h (118.5 mph) in 2006 (statistics courtesy of IBM)—but the serve has also become more accurate, making players increasingly harder to beat when they get a high percentage of first serves into court. This is highlighted when we consider the first serve statistics of the four Grand Slam winners in 2006 (Amelie Mauresmo at the Australian Open and Wimbledon, Justine Henin-Hardenne at the French Open, and Maria Sharapova at the US Open). In Australia, Mauresmo won 75 percent of her first serve points and 78 percent at Wimbledon. In Paris, Henin-Hardenne won 70 percent, and in New York, Sharapova won 76 percent (statistics courtesy of IBM). All of these champions achieved notable success when using their first serve, and they used power and accuracy throughout.

Overall improvements in the first serve have developed as a result of physical and psychological factors. Physically, the professional female tennis player is becoming taller, stronger, and faster (for example, the average WTA top 10 player is now over 3 centimetres [1.2 inches] taller than in 1991). Psychologically, she is trying to hurt her opponent with the serve rather than simply starting the point with it. She recognises it as the first point of attack and therefore her chance to immediately impose her own specific game style. With its power and accuracy, the first serve is now the first shot in a winning pattern of play.

The first serve tactics discussed in this section include options for players who prefer to attack from the baseline (groundstroke attack), as well as for those who like to play at the net (sneak, drive volley, and volley). There is also advice for the player who does not attack with one specific shot, but rather, tries to maintain control with a series of groundstrokes after the serve (maintaining baseline control). Using the first serve in doubles is also discussed, along with the various options for court positioning and player movement after the serve has been hit.

First Serve and Groundstroke Attack

I would always try to attack my opponent after I hit a strong first serve—especially with my backhand groundstroke.

—Asa Svensson (née Carlsson), Former Swedish Number 1 and Top 30 WTA Tour Player

The most common first serve tactic on the women's singles tour is the serve and groundstroke attack. It is regularly used to dominate an opponent from the very start of the point and can be applied at any time during a match from either the deuce or advantage court. This attack consists of a powerful and well-placed first serve and is followed by the server hitting an aggressive second shot (i.e., the third shot of the rally), usually early and from inside the baseline to maintain pressure on the returner.

When using the first serve and groundstroke attack, the server must consider which type of return will allow her to hit her favourite second shot and choose the serve that has the most chance of producing this return. The quality of this serve (i.e., its power and accuracy) will dictate whether this favoured second shot is used effectively. For this reason, she must specifically practice this type of serve regularly. It is also helpful for the server to anticipate the direction of the return whenever possible. If she can do this, her second shot will be earlier and of a higher quality. As a rule, the more powerful and accurate the first serve is, the greater the chance the return has of being caught late and thus fading away from the intended target. For example, a strong first serve out wide from the advantage court to a right-hander's backhand is more likely to produce a slightly late return down the line or to the middle of the court than to produce a sharp-angle, crosscourt return. If this happens regularly in a match, then the right-handed server should begin to anticipate hitting a forehand as her second shot from this position. By contrast, the serve out wide from the deuce court will often force a return that fades toward the right-handed server's backhand. The ability to dictate and anticipate in this way is the key to dominating with the first serve and aggressive groundstroke attack.

Depending on the server's second shot preference, this tactic comes in two forms: the first serve and attacking forehand, and the first serve and early backhand. Players using the first serve and attacking forehand tactic may play their forehands from almost anywhere on the court, provided they are in an attacking position. When hitting forehands from her forehand side, the player should move straight to the ball. This direct movement is crucial in preventing the opponent from having time to recover. Players who move only sideways will often lose the initiative in the rally. The player should move around the ball when hitting forehands from her backhand side. She must create enough space around the ball to be able to hit with power and aggression.

Figures 1.1 and 1.2 show the right-handed server's forehand options following first serves down the middle of the court. In figure 1.1 the server hits a penetrating first serve down the middle from the advantage court. The return fades across the court to her backhand side, so from inside the baseline the server moves around the ball and hits either the 'inside-out' (crosscourt) or 'inside-in' forehand (down the line; see chapter 2 for an explanation) from this position. This shot doesn't have to be hit close to the lines if it is hit with enough power from an aggressive position. The pace and time pressure applied will be enough to dominate the returner. In figure 1.2 the server hits a first serve down the middle from the deuce court. The return fades across the court to her forehand side, and the server moves straight to the ball to hit either crosscourt or down the line. Again, power and an aggressive court position are crucial to this tactic. In both of these tactics, the same principle applies to the left-handed server, except that the movement *around* the ball occurs in the deuce court and the movement *to* the ball occurs in the advantage court. Note the different types of movement needed for these forehands. The inside-out/inside-in forehand requires the player to *create* a space around the ball, whereas the forehand on the run

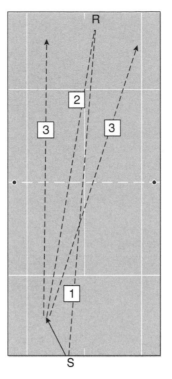

FIGURE 1.1 Forehand options following a right-handed first serve down the middle from the advantage court.

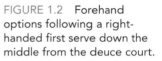

FIGURE 1.2 Forehand options following a right-handed first serve down the middle from the deuce court.

requires the player to move *into* a space to hit the ball. It is vital that the server practice both types of movement patterns.

🎾 Coaching Tip

An excellent exercise that helps a player practice her first serve tactics is to allow three serves per point instead of two. This gives the server two chances per point to construct a first serve pattern of play. If she misses the serve, she has the chance to correct her technique immediately—thus allowing valuable serving practice within a competitive situation.

The first serve and early backhand tactic applies to players who don't necessarily favour their forehand side but instead prefer to use their backhand to attack with. Whereas the attacking forehand can be hit from almost anywhere on the court, the early backhand following a strong first serve is hit early and from inside the baseline. This early contact can often be more important than pace or depth because it gives the returner virtually no time to recover. Even players who prefer their forehand may choose to use this tactic against a fast ball that is returned down the middle of the

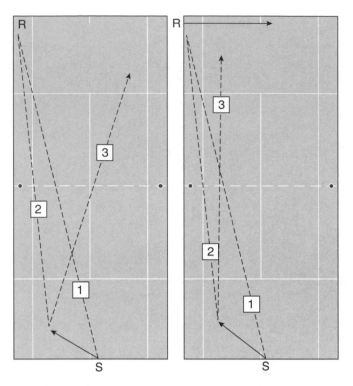

FIGURE 1.3 The crosscourt backhand following a wide first serve from the deuce court.

FIGURE 1.4 The wrong-footing backhand following a wide first serve from the deuce court.

court. In this situation, they may find that they have less time to prepare for a fore-hand (since the forehand uses a bigger swing), and so the backhand becomes a more effective option. Figures 1.3 and 1.4 show the right-handed server's options following the popular tactic of serving out wide from the deuce court in order to dictate with a backhand groundstroke. This serve is hit most effectively with slice. The server aims to hit around the outside edge of the ball to make the serve turn away from the returner—dragging her wide of the court. In figure 1.3 the wide first serve results in a return that fades away, either down the line or down the middle of the court. This allows the right-hander to step up and hit her backhand early into the space crosscourt. Figure 1.4 shows the same shot construction but with the server opting to hit her second shot back behind her opponent, thus wrong-footing her as she moves to the middle of the court. Note that the same tactic applies to the left-hander who hits the first serve out wide from the advantage court.

To practice the tactics discussed in this section, see drills 1.1 through 1.5 on pages 28 through 32.

🎾 Coaching Tip

Serving targets are often used to measure the accuracy of a serve and provide a visual record for the player. However, it is important to be able to measure the power of a serve also (without needing a speed gun!). This can be done by placing a marker where the serve's second bounce lands. If the serve hits the back fence before its second bounce, then the coach measures how high up the fence the ball hits. This 'power marker' should rise (or lengthen) with an increase in serving pace.

The first serve and groundstroke attack tactic is commonly used in doubles. According to Brent Larkham of Tennis Australia, the majority of female players stay back after their serve (less than 50 percent of women on the WTA Tour serve and volley in doubles compared to over 75 percent of men on the ATP Tour). A powerful first serve is backed up by an aggressive groundstroke hit down the line—straight at the returner's partner. This is an aggressive, planned tactic that is used effectively against a weak net player. Figure 1.5 shows how a doubles team would use the serve and groundstroke attack tactic. In figure 1.5 the right-handed server hits a first serve down the middle from the deuce court. The return fades back across the court to her forehand side, and she moves straight to the ball and hits her second shot aggressively down the line. Note how the server's partner is looking to cover the middle of the court in anticipation of a defensive volley played from her opponent at the net. The same tactic would apply when serving from the advantage court also. The server's partner must know beforehand that this is what the server is planning to do, because it allows her to cover the middle of the court in anticipation of a weak volley.

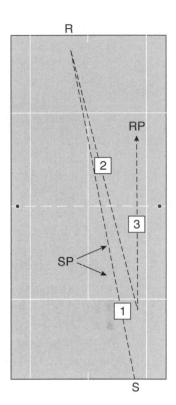

FIGURE 1.5 The right-hander's forehand ground-stroke attack down the line following a first serve down the middle from the deuce court.

First Serve and Baseline Control

Sometimes the server wants to maintain control over her opponent but does not have a planned shot to hit after a strong first serve. This could be because the return has been hit deep down the middle of the court (reducing the angle and space available for the server's second shot). It could also be that the server doesn't necessarily have the ability to dominate an opponent immediately (the return may have been played to her weaker side, for example). This tactic is particularly relevant to junior players who need more shots to create an attacking position because they don't hit the ball with as much power.

In other words, the serve and baseline control tactic involves the server working gradually toward a winning position, rather than setting up this position within two shots. In this scenario, the server's plan should be to dominate by hitting a number of quality groundstrokes that eventually open up a space, force a short ball, or pressure the opponent into an error. The key to this tactic is maintaining control. The server doesn't necessarily try to hit an immediate winner from her second shot, but works on increasingly dominating her opponent as the rally goes on while trying not to allow her opponent the chance to regain a neutral position at any time during the point.

To practice maintaining control after the first serve, see drill 1.6 on page 33.

Coaching Tip

Servers should be wary of players who hit the backhand slice as their preferred choice of return. The pace of the first serve can be controlled more easily when the returner uses a short, compact swing. The slice return is often hit accurately and low and can be difficult to attack. In this situation it is worth considering the serve to the forehand because there is more chance of a higher-bouncing, 'pacier' return, which may be easier to maintain control against.

In doubles, a serving team will often want to maintain control over a returning team by using a series of high-quality groundstrokes. Instead of using the attacking groundstroke down the line as a second shot, the server hits crosscourt while her partner at the net looks to intercept a weak reply with a winning volley. The better the crosscourt groundstroke is, the more chance the server's partner has of finishing the point from the net. Figure 1.6 shows the tactical intent of the serving team when the server maintains control of the point from the baseline. In this figure, a first serve from the advantage court is followed by a series of crosscourt groundstrokes between the server and returner. Once the server gains control of the rally, her partner looks to intercept with

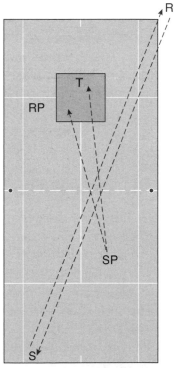

FIGURE 1.6 Serving and maintaining control of the baseline from the advantage court.

a winning volley into the shaded target area. Note how the intercept volley target area is positioned in the middle of the court. This allows for a high margin of error (i.e., the shot is a relatively safe one because it is hit into a big target area, allowing room for error). It also means that the volley is hit down to the feet or behind the returner's partner, making it very difficult to defend against. Note also that the server's partner moves forward toward the ball she is about to volley. This movement allows her to hit more aggressively.

First Serve and Drive Volley

A newly established tactic used in the women's game by players such as the Williams sisters is the serve and drive volley. A powerful first serve can force a high, defensive return. If this return is allowed to bounce, the initiative can be lost because the returner has time to recover. Also, it is harder to generate pace off a slow, deep, bouncing ball. Therefore, just as with the early, aggressive groundstroke tactics, the server should recognise the high, defensive return as a chance to maintain dominance and hit her second shot out of the air as a drive volley.

The drive volley differs from the normal volley in that it is hit using groundstroke technique. In other words, the player swings through the ball rather than punching through it, thus creating more pace and spin on the ball. This extra pace is required because the drive volley is often hit from behind the service line and against the high, floated return. Because the ball has little pace itself, the server must add pace to it. Players choose to drive volley the floating ball because they believe that the added pace and spin allows them to control the shot better than with a blocked volley, especially when it is played from above shoulder height.

The lack of time allowed to the returner is the key to this tactic's success. This is an important point. The returner will often not be in a position to defend against the drive volley because she is not ready in time. As a result, her movement will be less effective, and she may end up guessing which side to defend, allowing the target area for the server's second shot to remain large. This drive volley should therefore be played with a big margin for error (i.e., comfortably within the lines) because lack of time beats the returner.

To practice the first serve and drive volley tactic, see drill 1.7 on page 34.

The drive volley is also hit as a server's second shot in doubles when a high return floats out of the reach of the server's partner at the net. The server, quickly reading the flight path of the oncoming ball, moves inside the baseline and hits an aggressive drive volley either crosscourt to the returner on the baseline or down the line to the returner's partner at the net. This shot helps the serving team maintain dominance over the returning team for the same reasons as it does for the serving singles player.

First Serve and Sneak

Coaches often encourage their players to 'sneak' when rallying, so why not do this after a good first serve? If the server sees the return floating or short, she should try to take the return out of the air by sneaking (or 'ghosting') in to the net. Like the first serve and drive volley, the first serve and sneak is an instinctive tactic based on the effectiveness of the serve. This means that the player makes her decision after her first serve rather than before it. (This differs from the traditional serve and volley tactic, described next, in which the server decides to come in behind her serve before the point starts.)

The difference between the first serve and sneak and the first serve and drive volley is that the drive volley will be hit against the high, floating return, whereas the sneak volley will be hit against the lower return. This will either be an orthodox volley or, if the return falls very close to the net, a short, 'put-away' groundstroke. Although this uses a groundstroke, the server has still used the sneak tactic to play it.

To practice using the sneak after the first serve, see drill 1.8 on page 35.

The sneak volley is also hit by the server as a second shot in doubles when the returner is under pressure from the serve. In a similar way in which the drive volley is hit, if the return gets past the server's partner at the net, then the sneak volley becomes an option for the server if she is quick enough to react. This is an important tactic for the server to use (even if she plays most of her service points from the baseline) because it shows her opponents that she is prepared to play from the net at any time. This variety in play prevents her opponents from feeling too comfortable on the return. If the server plays only from the baseline, then the players on the returning team know that as long as they return away from the net player, they will have time to regain a good court position after the serve. Indeed, even if the server misses her sneak volley, she may have still planted an important element of doubt in the returning team's mind.

First Serve and Volley

When serving we usually plan the point as to where we will serve, what formation we will use, and what the server's partner at the net will do—i.e., will she intercept with a volley, fake, or stay.

—Cara Black, Two-Time Wimbledon Doubles Champion (2004 and 2005)

The serve and volley tactic differs from the drive volley and sneak volley tactics because it is planned rather than instinctual. In other words, the server decides before the point to approach the net behind her serve—no matter what! This tactic is being used less in women's singles today because the strength of the return and passing shot has improved dramatically in recent years. Almost every player loves to have a physical target to aim for, and this is what a player at the net provides. Therefore, the serve and volley tactic is now being used more as a way of mixing up the play than anything else. Indeed, some players use this tactic extremely well. Amelie Mauresmo provided a great example of this when she won her first Wimbledon title, in 2006, by predominantly serve and volleying in the latter stages of the tournament. Her opponents were simply not used to playing against this tactic, especially on the fast-bouncing grass courts that allowed them little time to prepare for their shots.

There are some key situations in which the serve and volley tactic can be used effectively. The first is using the wide slice serve on fast courts to force a 'blocked' return, which can be volleyed. Some double-handers are forced into blocking returns when the serve is hit wide of them with a low bounce. Left-handed servers, in particular, use this tactic well when serving from the advantage court to the right-handed returner. The low slice serve is also effective against players who use extreme grips because they find it harder to get the racket face underneath a low ball, thereby forcing the blocked return. This return usually floats higher and slower than the topspin return does, making it easier to volley against. The slower pace allows the server to move closer in to the net before playing the volley, and the lack of spin means that the volley is played at a more comfortable height than a topspin return, which could dip down to the volleyer's feet.

The second situation in which the serve and volley tactic can be used effectively is using a high and wide topspin serve to force a blocked return. Most women are unable to execute this type of serve because of the considerable strength this shot requires. However, against the single-handed backhand returner, a 'kick' topspin serve may be high and wide enough to prevent the returner from hitting 'over the top' of the ball, resulting in a block that is relatively easy to volley against.

The third situation is serving and volleying against players who always slice their backhand return. This sliced shot can start to float a little over the course of a match, and if so, this return should be attacked! This tactic also introduces an element of surprise into play. It prevents the returner from feeling too comfortable because she is forced to watch her opponent as well as the ball.

Figure 1.7 shows the serve and volley tactic being played from the advantage court. In this figure, the server comes in behind a wide serve to the advantage court. The blocked return fades down the line, allowing the server to hit a winning volley into the open court. Note how the server follows the line of her serve and moves inside the service line before hitting the volley, thus allowing the returner as little time as possible to recover for her next shot.

To practice the serve and volley tactic, see drill 1.9 on page 36.

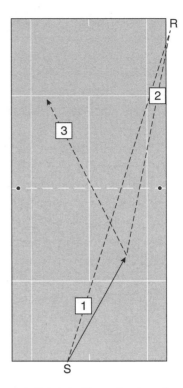

FIGURE 1.7 The volley into the space following a first serve out wide from the advantage court.

Although the majority of players serve and stay back, many top doubles players throughout the modern era, such as Martina Navratilova, Lisa Raymond, and Cara Black, have used the serve and volley tactic with great success. The doubles format allows players to serve and volley more often because of the limited target space given to the returner (i.e., a half court in doubles compared to a whole court in singles). As a result, specific patterns of play with planned movement of the serving team centred on the serve and volley tactic are commonly used.

In doubles, the majority of serve and volley tactics are based around the serve down the middle of the court. In fact, it is the middle of the court in general that good doubles pairs try to control. The middle serve allows the returner less angle to work with and gives the server's partner the best chance to control the net. This serve also takes away the right-hander's backhand crosscourt return from the advantage court—widely recognised as one of the most effective returns on the women's tour.

The server's partner must know the direction of the serve in advance so she can anticipate the most likely return and position herself accordingly. Generally, good doubles players like to position themselves quite centrally (i.e., closer to the centre line than the sideline) and move diagonally forward and inward following the middle serve. They move forward and outward following a wide serve in anticipation of a late return hit down the line, allowing their partner to move in and cover the middle of the court.

Figures 1.8 and 1.9 show the different types of movement patterns made by the serving team following a first serve hit wide and down the middle. In figure 1.8 a first serve hit wide to the deuce court results in the serving team covering the line and middle return. The server's partner moves forward and outward to cover the line, and the server moves forward and toward the middle to cover the centre. Note how their movements are coordinated, and how the server's partner moves forward as well as outward. In figure 1.9 a first serve hit down the middle from the advantage court results in the serving team covering the middle and crosscourt return. This time the server's partner moves forward and inward to cover the middle, and the server covers the remainder of the court. In this situation the server's partner must not move too early; otherwise, she will open a space down her line for the returner to hit into.

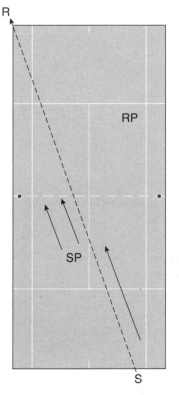

FIGURE 1.8 The serve and volley tactic using the first serve hit wide to the deuce court.

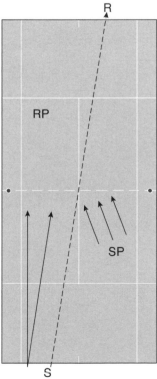

FIGURE 1.9 The serve and volley tactic using the first serve hit down the middle from the advantage court.

The I formation and Australian formation are two commonly used doubles plays that are based around the serve and volley tactic. They are most effective when used with the serve down the middle from either the deuce or advantage court. The I formation sees the server's partner take a completely central position on the court (crouching low so as not to be hit by the serve). The server hits the serve from a central court position also, rather than a traditional wide position on the baseline, thus creating an I formation between the server and her partner. This tactic allows the server's partner to take complete control of the centre of the net and helps to neutralise the threat of the crosscourt return. Figures 1.10 and 1.11 show the I formation being used from both the deuce and advantage courts. Figure 1.10 shows the I formation being used with a first serve hit down the middle from the deuce court. The server takes up a central serving position on the baseline, almost directly behind her partner, who is taking up a similar central position at the net. The server follows her serve in and covers the line return. Her partner covers the middle and crosscourt return. Figure 1.11 shows the I formation being used with a first serve hit down the middle from the advantage court. Again, the server uses the serve and volley tactic and covers the return down the line, leaving her partner to cover the middle and crosscourt return (the two most likely returns from this

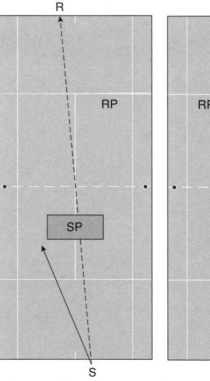

FIGURE 1.10 The I formation used with a middle serve hit from the deuce court.

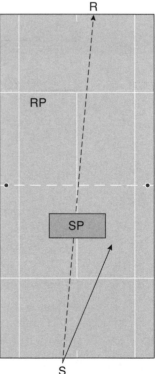

FIGURE 1.11 The I formation used with a middle serve hit from the advantage court.

serve). The server's partner must hold her position when playing the I formation with a middle serve because this allows her to maintain control of the centre of the court. Some players automatically move to the left or right (covering the opposite side to their partners), but this often leaves a big gap down the middle—the most important place to cover! Note how the server's central serving position changes the angle of her serve, often allowing for a more accurate middle serve to be hit. The I formation can also be used with a wide serve with either the server or her partner choosing to cover the return hit down the line. These formations, using varied, planned movement from both players, will often unsettle the rhythm of the returning team because they are not given the same visual target to aim for each time.

The Australian formation is used when trying to neutralise an extreme threat from a crosscourt return. This requires the server's partner to stand on the same half of the court as the server—directly in the line of the crosscourt return. Figure 1.12 shows the Australian doubles formation being used with a middle serve hit from the advantage court. Note how the server's partner is positioned on the same side of the court as the server, so she is well placed to receive the crosscourt return. The server uses the serve and volley tactic and covers the return hit down the line. Note how the middle serve reduces the angle available to the returner also. The same formation is used on the deuce court to neutralise the threat of the crosscourt return.

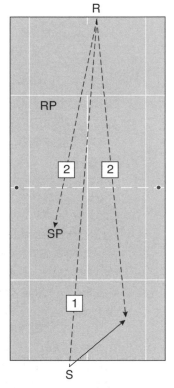

The key to executing any of these tactics successfully lies in good communication within the serving pair. The server's partner must know the direction of the serve in advance, as well as the area of the net that her partner is going to cover. Both players' roles should

FIGURE 1.12 **The Australian formation used from the advantage court.**

be clearly defined. This attention to detail separates the great doubles teams from the rest. To develop this detail, doubles teams should practice specific set plays repeatedly so they are constantly refining their movement patterns, shot selection, and communication. Players should be prepared to play full practice sets using one specific tactic to build confidence with it.

To practice the serve and volley tactic as a serving team, see drill 1.10 on page 37.

Coaching Tip

In the middle of a practice session, the coach can ask the players to stop what they're doing and immediately try to hold one service game against their practice partner (provided they have warmed up serves beforehand). This is a good intervention drill that helps to remind players that it is important to try to hold serve in any situation. Players may feel uncomfortable doing this to begin with because they may not be fully prepared—but this is exactly the point of the drill!

The Effective Second Serve

The second serve remains an area of weakness in the women's game. Statistics tend to support this view. In the four Grand Slams of 2006, the percentage of second serve points won in the women's singles events was 41 percent (based on 508 matches played), which compares unfavourably with the men, who won around 47 percent of theirs (statistics courtesy of IBM). This 6 percent difference becomes fairly substantial over the course of a tightly contested match. More important, these statistics clearly show that if a server is making a low percentage of first serves, then the returner quickly becomes the favourite to win.

The second serve differs primarily from the first serve because the server must make this shot in the court. As a result, the second serve is usually hit more conservatively, with more spin, less pace, and often less accuracy. This combination simply makes it easier to attack. The following sections outline ways the server can make her second serve more potent—with accuracy and variety of direction being critical factors. Although these aspects apply as much to the first serve as to the second serve, their tactical use in making the second serve effective is significant here.

Accuracy

A class second serve has a rock solid foundation, yet always keeps the opponent guessing.

—Nigel Sears, Former Coach to WTA Top 10 Players Daniela Hantuchova and Amanda Coetzer

Most top women players do not defend with extremely powerful second serves. Instead, they tend to reduce the pace on the ball in favour of adding more spin, making it a safer shot. As a result, the accuracy of the serve assumes a more critical role, and this will often decide which player can attack first in the point. Indeed, there is no reason why an accurate second serve shouldn't counter the threat of the returner and create an attacking opportunity for the server instead. Maria Sharapova, for example, doesn't hit a very fast second serve, but she does maintain pinpoint accuracy. Her second serve down the middle from the deuce court often crosses the net to the right of the net strap (as she faces it), yet lands to the left of the centre line. She must maintain this level of accuracy; otherwise, her serve will sit nicely in the forehand hitting zone of the right-handed returner.

To improve the accuracy of her second serve, a player must be prepared to miss it sometimes! She must hit this shot with courage and confidence because often she will be better off making an error that lands close to the line than pushing the ball into the middle of the service box. This shot will inevitably be attacked by the returner, boosting the returner's own feelings of confidence and dominance if successful. Hitting an accurate second serve, whether in or (just) out, can often force the returner to step back and play a more neutral return next time.

To practice the tactics discussed in this section, see drills 1.11 and 1.12 on pages 37 and 38.

Variety of Direction

It is crucial for a player to be able to vary the direction of her second serve, as well as maintain its accuracy, if she is to cope with an aggressive returner. Maintaining this variety will prevent her opponent from settling into a consistent returning rhythm. The most successful female servers do this to great effect. They have the ability to serve to both sides of their opponents (i.e., to both the opponents' weak and strong sides) as well as into their bodies, while analysing their technical and tactical capabilities along the way. This simply means that they will quickly figure out the returner's least effective return, and play to it accordingly!

Weaker Versus Stronger Side   Serving to an opponent's backhand side on the second serve is usually encouraged in the junior game because, at a very young age, this is often the weaker side. However, this policy does not necessarily follow in the pros because the backhand is not always an opponent's weak side. Many players prefer to hit returns on the backhand. The majority of players now play with two hands on the backhand side, which enables them to absorb pace more easily than single-handers, because the extra hand provides more strength. Also, because of this extra strength, the double-hander can afford to hit with a contact point closer to her body, which means she requires less time to prepare for the shot than the single-hander, whose contact point is farther in front because the swing is longer. As a result, the double-handed backhand return has become widely recognised as one of the most effective shots hit on the tour today.

It is important to remember, however, that the double-handed returner has less reach on the wide ball than her single-handed counterpart does. If the server can serve beyond her reach, then the threat of the return can be nullified—especially if the returner struggles to move well to this side. The single-handed backhand opponent, on the other hand, may find the serve that turns into her body more difficult to deal with because of her longer swing.

There are some interesting tactical reasons for serving to an opponent's stronger returning side, as opposed to serving to her weaker side. If an opponent has a stronger backhand than forehand, for example, hitting a wide serve to the backhand (from the advantage court to a right-hander and from the deuce court to a left-hander) will allow the server the chance to expose the weaker forehand side with her second shot. The width of the serve will open up the court so the server can hit her next shot into the space, forcing her opponent to hit her weaker forehand on the run. The same principle would be used against a stronger forehand side, the only difference being that the wide serve would be used from the opposite court. This tactic is possible as long as the server isn't under too much pressure from the return! Figure 1.13 shows a second serve hit wide from the deuce court to the stronger forehand side of this right-handed opponent. The server is forcing her opponent to hit her weaker backhand on the run by hitting her second shot down the line. This tactic will prove successful if the server gains enough width on her serve (pulling her opponent off the court) and is in a good enough position after serving to hit her second shot down the line.

Another reason to serve to a returner's strong side is that some players like to use an opponent's pace of shot to create pace for themselves (a tactic called counterpunching). This tactic is used effectively as

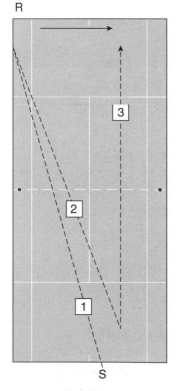

FIGURE 1.13 The second serve hit out wide from the deuce court to an opponent's strength.

long as the server is able to move quickly to the aggressive return and hit just as aggressively back. The server's court position must remain close to the baseline, and her technique must be executed efficiently if she is to put enough time and pace pressure on the returner.

Some experienced players will choose to serve to an opponent's stronger side on a less important point—for example, at 40–0 or 40–15 up. In other words, they will give an opponent her favourite shot in return for maintaining variety. This will allow them to serve more effectively to the weaker side on the really big points. Finally, there is an important psychological reason why a player may choose to serve and play to her opponent's obvious strength. If a player can do this successfully, she stands a good chance of breaking her opponent's belief in her own game. This is because if the opponent cannot win with her strengths, what chance does she have of winning with her weaknesses?

To practice the tactics discussed in this section, see drills 1.13 and 1.14 on pages 39 and 40.

Body Serve   The serving direction being used increasingly in the women's game today is the serve into the body. As the female athlete becomes taller, quicker, and stronger, her ability to execute shots from either side of her body also improves. The opponent with long limbs and a wide reach will often prefer to return a ball that is hit away from her body rather than a ball that 'cramps' her technique by being hit too close to her. This applies, in particular, to an opponent using the single-handed topspin backhand return. This shot requires more space because it is hit with a longer swing and a contact point farther in front of the body than the double-handed backhand. (From a technical perspective, it is hit with more 'linear' momentum—that is, through the ball in a longer line—compared to the double-handed shot, which uses more 'angular' momentum—that is, a more rotational movement.) As a result, the single-handed backhand tends to require more precise positioning, which the body serve can often hinder.

The body serve also reduces the angles available to the returner. This is usually a more important factor for the second serve than the first because it is more likely to be attacked. The wider the serve is, the more acute the crosscourt angle becomes. For this reason, the returner must be put under enough pressure to prevent her from dominating from this wide position. With fewer angles available to her from the body serve, the returner may try to force an angled shot (which may not actually exist) and make an error. Therefore, the body serve helps to reduce the attacking space available for an opponent.

To practice the body serve, see drill 1.15 on page 40.

Pace and Rhythm

If the second serve is being continually dominated, it can sometimes help for the server to vary the pace by suddenly hitting a 'big' second serve (i.e., significantly increasing the pace of the serve). Even if she misses the shot, this sudden injection of aggressive energy can instantly change the momentum of a match, sending the message that the server is prepared to 'fight her way out of her corner'. Making just one simple adjustment for only one point of the match may be enough to decrease an opponent's belief in her return. It could force her to start looking out for the next big second serve and assuming a more defensive returning position in the process. Sometimes reducing the pace of the serve increases its effectiveness. This tactic could be used against an opponent who thrives on pace and who finds it harder to generate pace herself. Substituting pace for more spin, for example, may prove to be a great tactical solution.

Varying the pace of the second serve can often surprise an opponent and change the momentum of a match.

Varying the rhythm of the second serve can help take back the initiative. For example, by taking more time between serves, a player can unsettle an aggressive returner who likes to play quickly. This tactic can be employed to good effect when the server uses her full time allocation between points. Similarly, a server who varies her pre-point routine can often unsettle a returner's rhythm. For example, varying the number of times she bounces the ball before serving will make it harder for the returner to prepare consistently. However, the server must be careful not to unsettle her own rhythm in the process!

Spin

In the men's game both slice and topspin second serves are commonly used on the tour. Men have more upper- and lower-body strength than women have and generally have longer 'levers' and wider shoulders than women do. These physical qualities give them faster and stronger body segments to use when serving, which, in turn, creates more significant amounts of topspin when required. This is not the case in the women's game because fewer female players possess the strength required to produce such topspin. The slice second serve is therefore used far more often than the topspin because it requires less physical strength to execute effectively. This lack of serving variety in women's tennis causes the second serve to become much more predictable to return. Players and coaches therefore face an important decision when choosing the type of spin to use in developing the second serve.

As previously mentioned, although most servers can successfully use the slice, very few women currently use topspin second serves on the WTA Tour. Justine Henin-Hardenne, Sam Stosur, and Alicia Molik are a few of the players who can hit this serve effectively. A topspin serve hit without strength will often 'sit up' at an ideal height for a returner to attack. This is especially true when serving down the middle from the deuce court for right-handers and the advantage court for left-handers. The danger with the topspin second serve is that most players can now attack the high bouncing ball with ease. This is especially true for women with double-handed backhands. These players use the strength of both arms to 'command' the ball and are able to hit early and aggressively. In fact, it is very rare for a woman to be able to hit a topspin second serve high and wide enough to force her opponent to play the shot from outside the singles court. This is the main reason the slice serve is proving more effective: It is much harder to attack a serve that stays low. Figure 1.14 shows how a weak topspin second serve hit out wide from the advantage court can be dominated by the returner. Note how the wide serve has created a natural space for the returner to hit into—either crosscourt or down the line.

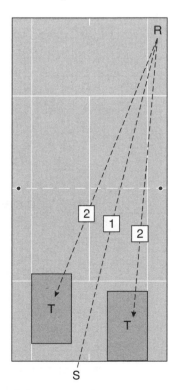

FIGURE 1.14 Returning options against the topspin second serve hit out wide from the advantage court.

The slice second serve is particularly effective on fast courts and against opponents with extreme grips who find it hard to get 'underneath' the ball when it stays low. The movement that the slice brings to the ball can also cause problems for opponents because it forces them to hit up over the net rather than allowing them to hit down into the court. It is, therefore, probably the server's best chance to neutralise the returner's advantage. Indeed, an aggressive slice serve hit either down the middle, into the body, or out wide can be more effective than a topspin serve that can't pull an opponent out of her optimal hitting zone. Figure 1.15 shows how a middle or body slice second serve from the advantage court can reduce the angles available to the returner. Note how the returner's target area is much more central compared to the topspin serve out wide. This allows the server more chance to neutralise the rally with her second shot.

The issue of which spins to use on the second serve must be seriously considered. Some coaches insist that their players can hit both the slice and the topspin. Players who can do this will hold a real advantage over their fellow competitors—but they are rare.

To practice the tactics discussed in this section, see drills 1.16 and 1.17 on pages 41 and 42.

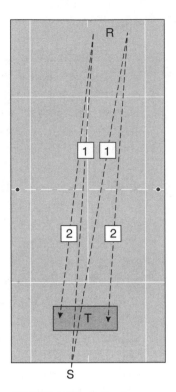

FIGURE 1.15 Returning options against the slice second serve hit down the middle or into the body from the advantage court.

Doubles players face the same challenges as the singles player does in terms of using the second serve effectively. Again, containing the threat of an aggressive returning team is crucial and requires sound tactical planning and a proactive, positive approach. The key to containing this threat lies in preventing the returning team from finding a consistent returning rhythm. This is done by varying the serve direction and varying each player's movement patterns at the net.

Using a combination of slice serves hit down the middle and into the body (to reduce the angles available to the returner) is a good tactic no matter which movement pattern is being used. The slice serve will help to keep the ball low and will be harder to attack.

Crucially, the server's partner must still look to intercept as much as possible. This is not easy because many players believe that they can only really intercept on their partner's first serve. Players must be more proactive in this situation and be prepared to take some risks to keep the returning team guessing. This is especially true when it comes to playing the big points. At 30–40 the returner is more likely to play her return crosscourt (choosing the higher-percentage return on an important point), so why not plan to intercept this with a volley? The psychological effect that this kind of play will have on the returning team is immense, because a seed of doubt is sown even if the point is lost.

Paying close attention to the opponents' returning habits will be a great help also. For example, noting when and how often the returning team hits down the line against the second serve is crucial to staying in control of the game. If an opponent hits down the line only occasionally, then intercepting with a volley on her next return is a smart play because she is most likely to return crosscourt again. If the returner continually hits down the line off the second serve, the server's partner would consider adjusting her position closer to the sideline as a consequence. If the opponent uses the aggressive lob down the line, then the server's partner may reposition slightly farther back from the net. Picking up on these habits can give the serving team an extra edge that might help them win a greater proportion of crucial second serve points.

Left-Handed Servers

For years coaches have speculated on the advantage of being a left-handed server. The way the serve moves with slice away from the right-hander's backhand can cause problems, especially because there aren't many left-handed servers to practice against. This is the key. The left-handed serve is awkward because it is less familiar.

The wide serve hit from the advantage court is often the most difficult to return. The movement of the ball away from the returner drags her position wide of the singles court, leaving the rest of the court exposed. The lefty server uses this to great effect considering the fact that six out of eight game point situations are played out from the advantage side (40–0, 40–30, Adv–in, 0–40, 30–40, Adv–out). However, she must be careful not to use this wide serve too often as a second serve. If the returner begins to anticipate the direction of this serve, then the server will leave herself open to an angled attack crosscourt or into the space down the line.

Therefore, a good left-handed server should also have the ability to hit the serve down the middle from the advantage court. The left-hander should also practice the flat wide serve from the deuce court. Patty Schnyder (an excellent left-handed WTA pro player) does this exceptionally well because she knows that her slice middle serve from this side will not cause the right-handed returner quite as many problems because her court position remains central.

For second serve points, the left-handed server should consider using the serve into the body on a regular basis. As mentioned earlier, the movement of the serve from a left-hander is less familiar. A slice second serve will move in a left to right direction rather than a right to left direction, meaning that a body serve will be hit in the direction of a right-handed returner's *forehand* before sliding closer in to her body, compared to the right-handed serve that is hit initially in the direction of the backhand. This difference in direction is crucial because the forehand return usually requires a bigger swing, more space, and more preparation time than the backhand return (especially the double-handed backhand). As a result, the left-handed body serve will often cramp a right-handed returner very effectively, particularly when the returner tries to create space for her forehand. In effect, the ball 'chases' in toward the body of a right-handed opponent. For advice to the right-hander on how to counter this advantage, see chapter 2.

Serving Percentages

Perhaps the most effective way of playing against a dominant returner is simply to prevent her from hitting many second serve returns! This means the server needs to get a high percentage of first serves into court—usually around 60 to 65 percent. However, this percentage may need to be higher if the second serve is being punished. Even if some pace or accuracy is sacrificed, the returner usually brings a less aggressive returning mentality to the court when facing a first serve compared to a second serve. As a result, her returning position will usually be more defensive (i.e., she will stand slightly farther back), and this may just be enough to allow the server the chance to hold serve more easily.

The effectiveness of the serve can be measured in a number of ways, and these statistics can provide very valuable feedback. Coaches, parents, and players should experiment by charting the percentage of first and second serves in, as well as the points won on the first and second serves; the points won when serving to the forehand, backhand, and body; and the number of aces, double faults, and unreturned serves. In doing this, players can begin to build a picture of their own serving strengths and weaknesses, which, in turn, will lead them to establish their own individual game style. It will also encourage them to assess the strengths and weaknesses of their opponents in terms of which tactics proved most successful, enhancing their tactical awareness overall. For more on developing an individual game style, see chapter 6.

Figure 1.16 is a serving summary. To calculate the various percentage statistics that help indicate a player's serving performance, divide the first number in the sequence by the second number and multiply by 100.

Serving Summary

_____ (number of first serves in) / _____ (number of first serve attempts)

= _____ percentage of first serves in

_____ (number of second serves in) / _____ (number of second serve attempts)

= _____ percentage of second serves in

_____ (number of first serve points won) / _____ (total number of first serve points)

= _____ percentage of first serve points won

_____ (number of second serve points won) / _____ (total number of second serve points)

= _____ percentage of second serve points won

_____ (number of points won to forehand, backhand, body) / _____ (total number of points to forehand, backhand, body)

= _____ percentage of points won to forehand, backhand, body

_____ (number of unreturned serves) / _____ (total number of serve points)

= _____ percentage of unreturned serve points

Number of aces _____

Number of double faults _____

FIGURE 1.16 Serving summary.

Summary

☐ With its continual increase in accuracy and power, the first serve is now recognised as being the first point of attack for many female players. It provides a chance to immediately impose a specific game style on an opponent, and should be developed as the first shot in a winning pattern of play.

☐ The most common first serve tactic is the serve and groundstroke attack. This requires a powerful and well-placed first serve to be followed up by an aggressive second shot, usually hit early and from inside the baseline. The server can choose to hit this second shot as either a forehand or backhand, depending on her court position and the direction of the return. In doubles, this second shot is often hit down the line—straight at the returner's partner at the net.

☐ Sometimes the server wants to maintain control over her opponent but does not have a planned shot to hit after a strong first serve. In this scenario, the server will use the serve and baseline control tactic, in which she dominates by hitting a number of quality groundstrokes that eventually open up a space, force a short ball, or pressure the opponent into an error. Similarly in doubles, the server will look to control a crosscourt baseline rally so her partner can try to win the point with an intercept volley at the net.

☐ The serve and drive volley, and the serve and sneak tactic both involve the server making an instinctive decision to play a volley after an aggressive serve. The drive volley will usually be hit against the high, defensive return, whereas the sneak volley will be hit against the lower one. Both of these tactics apply equally to singles and doubles play.

☐ The serve and volley tactic is an excellent way of mixing up the play and can be used, in particular, when the serve forces a defensive, blocked return, which is easy to volley against. It could also be used against an opponent whose slice backhand return tends to float too much.

☐ In doubles, the majority of serve and volley tactics are based around the serve down the middle of the court. The I formation and Australian formation are positional options that allow the players on the serving team the chance to play to their strengths, as well as to exploit their opponents' weaknesses.

☐ Second serve tactics are usually based on the need to neutralise the threat posed by the returner. By achieving this, the server gives herself a chance to dominate the point instead.

☐ Most top female players do not defend with extremely powerful second serves, but use accuracy and variety as weapons instead. This includes using the serve into the body, using the wide serve, and deliberately serving to an opponent's stronger side to expose her weaker side with the second shot. When executing these tactics, female players use the slice serve far more than the topspin serve.

☐ In doubles, the serving team faces the same challenges as the singles player does in terms of neutralising the threat of the return. The key lies in preventing the returning team from finding a consistent returning rhythm. Using the middle and body serve will prove effective, as will encouraging the server's partner to intercept as much as possible—even against a second serve return (because the returning team will not expect this). Paying close attention to opponents' returning habits will also help when planning these movement patterns.

☐ The left-handed server holds an advantage over her right-handed opponent because her serve is less familiar. A good left-handed server should have the ability to hit the serve down the middle from the advantage court, in particular. This will prevent the returner from anticipating the wide serve too often.

☐ Hitting a high percentage of first serves in is another way of preventing the returner from dominating with her second serve return. Players should generally aim for getting between 60 and 65 percent of their first serves in.

DRILL 1.1 Hitting the Attacking Forehand After a First Serve

AIM
To practice the movement patterns needed to hit the attacking forehand after the first serve.

LEVEL
Intermediate to advanced

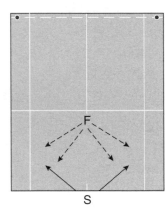

The server practices her movement to the attacking forehand.

DESCRIPTION
The player positions herself on the baseline as if she were about to serve (she should alternate between deuce court and advantage court serving positions). The coach stands facing the player inside the baseline on the same side of the court. The coach hand-feeds a short ball for the player to move to and hit as an attacking forehand. The player then returns to her serving position ready for the next ball, while facing the court at all times (copying the movement she would make in a match). The player completes the drill after moving to, and hitting, six forehands (three from each serving position). The coach should mix up the direction of the hand-feeds so the player can practice her movement straight to the ball as well as around the ball.

VARIATION
The coach increases the variety and amount of hand-feeds to include short, deep, and middle balls as the player progresses. The player then shadow-swings a serve before moving to hit each ball. In time, the coach moves to the opposite end of the court and feeds from the actual returning position. Practice progresses finally to the server hitting real serves before moving to hit her coach's feed.

COACHING POINTS
The coach should encourage the player to move straight to the ball when hitting forehands from her forehand side and to move around the ball when hitting forehands from her backhand side. Again, playing the shot from *inside* the baseline is vital. The player should have enough time to recover to the middle before the coach feeds the next ball (because she will be moving from this central position after serving).

DRILL 1.2   Dominating With the First Serve

AIMS
To practice the serve and groundstroke attack; to make the server select the best serve and second shot option; to make the server dominate the point.

LEVEL
Intermediate to advanced

DESCRIPTION
Two players play first to seven points with the same player serving until completion. The server has to win the point within three shots (including the first serve). If the server hasn't won the point after three shots, then the point stops immediately, and the returner wins the point. The server should try to hit her favourite second shot, and choose the serve that creates the best chance for this to happen. The players switch roles when finished.

VARIATION
If the server hasn't won the point after three shots, the point is allowed to finish. If the server wins the point after three shots, the server does not score, but does prevent the returner from scoring. If the returner wins the point after three shots, the returner scores a point as normal.

COACHING POINTS
Three shots from the server is quite a long rally in tennis (five or six shots in total, depending on whether the returner hits the final shot), so the coach should encourage the server to *construct* the point rather than rush to try to hit a winner. Some players find this drill uncomfortable. When the point ends after the server's third shot, the coach should note what type of position she is in. Is she dominating, or has the returner forced the upper hand? Her position at this moment in the rally will show how effective she is at using this tactic. It will highlight the serving sides or targets that she favours, as well as how dominant she is with her second shot.

DRILL 1.3   Holding Serve Even When the Opponent Knows the Tactic

This drill can be used to gauge a serve's quality. The server should still win the majority of the points if the serve is good enough.

AIMS
To show that a tactic's execution is more important than the variety of tactics used; to show that it may not matter whether the opponent knows or can anticipate the tactic in advance if the server can execute her serve and second shot well enough.

LEVEL
All

DESCRIPTION
Players play a practice set with the server telling the returner where she will hit her first serve before the start of each point. The server must play aggressively, trying to use the serve and groundstroke attack tactic whenever possible—yet without forcing her shots too much. She should still win her fair share of service points if she executes this tactic well enough, even though the returner knows where her serve is going.

VARIATIONS
1. A player who serves exceptionally well can try this drill with her second serve as well as her first.
2. To make the drill more realistic to an open point situation, the server tells the returner before the practice points begin where she will serve the majority of her first or second serves (or both).
3. The server tells the returner the direction of her serve only at key moments during practice points, to increase the pressure on herself (e.g., whenever she is down 15–30 in the game).

DRILL 1.4   Using Only Three First Serves per Game

AIM
To emphasise the value of getting a first serve in.

LEVEL
All

DESCRIPTION
Players play a practice set with the server being allowed to play only three first serve points per service game. The remaining points are played using second serves only. This may mean that the server doesn't actually get to play a first serve point if she misses all three attempts! The server must indicate to the returner—for instance, by 'showing' the ball as if using the 'new balls' sign—if she intends to use one of her first serves before the start of the point. This will allow the returner to adjust her returning position accordingly.

VARIATION
Only first serves *in* are counted toward the server's allocation of three. This allows the server more than three attempts if she needs them.

COACHING POINTS
The coach should note when the server chooses to use her first serves. In other words, does she use them when up, down, or at the start of each game? This will give a good indication as to how aware she is of the tactical momentum of the match and at what stage in the game she values her first serve most. Also, the coach should note whether she deliberately adjusts her first serve technique (e.g., adds more spin, slows the ball down) to get more in. This may indicate how important getting the serve in is to her, compared to hitting it aggressively.

DRILL 1.5 Using the First Serve to Create an Advantage

AIM
To highlight the quality of the serve, as well as the perception and anticipation skills of the server.

LEVEL
All

DESCRIPTION
Players play first to seven points with the same player serving until completion. The server has to be at least 60:40 up in the point (i.e., 60:40 favourite to win the point) as she is about to hit her second shot. If not, she loses the point immediately and catches the ball instead of hitting it. This means that the server has to dominate the returner by using a serve that creates an attacking opportunity straightaway. It also means that she has to read the tactical impact of her serve clearly and quickly to make the right decision.

VARIATIONS
1. The ratio of the server's position can be increased as the effectiveness of the serve improves (70:30, 80:20, etc.).
2. The coach sets performance targets for the server for every service game (e.g., she must hit at least one unreturnable serve per game or she starts at 0–15 in her next one).
3. The returner makes the decision instead of the server. This will give the server valuable feedback from her opponent's perspective.
4. The same drill is used for the second serve. The server must be at least 50:50 in the point as she is about to hit her second shot. Again, this ratio can be increased or decreased as appropriate.

COACHING POINTS
The coach should note what the server regards as being an advantageous position and how often she gets into one. This will highlight her tactical reading of the game and how effective her serve actually is.

DRILL 1.6   Maintaining Control After the First Serve

AIM
To maintain control over an opponent through a series of pressuring ground-strokes hit after the first serve.

LEVEL
All

DESCRIPTION
Players play first to seven points with the same player serving until completion. The server plays the point against the returner but only from the half of the court she served from. The returner plays in the whole court. The server hits her groundstrokes down the line and crosscourt, alternately, until the point is won. The return must be played back crosscourt to the server's half; otherwise, the point is lost immediately. The server plays from the half court to practice being in a dominant position, whereas the returner plays from the whole court to practice playing from a defensive position.

VARIATION
The server is allowed a certain amount of groundstrokes to construct with before the point is played out in the whole court for both players. For example, the server is allowed to hit four alternate shots (including the serve) before the returner can hit into the open court.

COACHING POINT
The coach should encourage the server to build pressure on the returner by hitting with consistency and accuracy so that a winning opportunity opens up naturally. The key here is to not allow the returner the chance to regain a neutral position at any time during the point.

DRILL 1.7   Using the Drive Volley After the First Serve

AIMS
To practice the first serve and drive volley tactic; to make the server dominate the point; to help the server improve her anticipation and perception skills.

LEVEL
Intermediate to advanced

DESCRIPTION
The server hits her first serve to predetermined targets. The coach returns the serve (or feeds a return if necessary) using a chipped, high ball that floats down the line or middle of the court. The server must hit her second shot as a drive volley. The player completes the drill after moving to and hitting six drive volleys (three from each serving position).

VARIATION
The coach feeds a variety of returns so the server has to decide quickly whether to hit the ball as a drive volley.

COACHING POINTS
The server must read the flight path of the ball quickly. She must decide whether to hit a forehand or backhand and move inside the baseline and position herself correctly. Again, a large target area should be encouraged for this shot.

DRILL 1.8   Using the Sneak After the First Serve

AIMS
To practice the first serve and sneak tactic; to make the server dominate the point; to help the server improve her anticipation and perception skills.

LEVEL
Intermediate to advanced

DESCRIPTION
The server hits her first serve to predetermined targets. The coach returns the serve in one of two ways: (1) hitting an attacking, topspin return or (2) hitting a sliced, more defensive return. The server must sneak in to the net against the sliced return. The player completes the drill after moving to, and hitting, five sneak volleys.

VARIATION
Players play points and receive bonuses when they use the serve and sneak tactic. The coach rewards the player's correct instinct, even if the point is lost.

COACHING POINTS
The server must be able to recognise two things quickly: (1) how her serve is going to affect the returner (anticipation) (i.e., as soon as the ball leaves her racket, she should have an idea as to how good the serve is going to be) and (2) the type of shot the returner has just played (perception) (i.e., is the return aggressive, defensive, or neutralising, and can it be volleyed?). The coach must match the return with the quality of the serve (e.g., a powerful and accurate serve should elicit a defensive return). This gives the player realistic and natural feedback.

DRILL 1.9   Practicing the Serve and Volley Tactic

AIMS
To practice the serve and volley tactic; to make the server dominate the point; to help the server improve her movement after the serve.

LEVEL
Intermediate to advanced

DESCRIPTION
Players play points to five with the server using first serves only to serve and volley with (i.e., they score only when the first serve goes in). The returner tries to make the server play every first volley by hitting back down the middle of the court. The server must hit her first volley from inside the service line; otherwise, she loses the point immediately. She is awarded three points for a winning volley, two points for winning the point using the serve and volley tactic, or one point if she makes her first volley into court but loses the point (thereby preventing her opponent from scoring). She is awarded one point if her opponent misses her return.

VARIATION
Players use normal tennis scoring but are awarded bonus points for smart use of the serve and volley tactic (even if the point is lost sometimes).

COACHING POINTS
The coach should encourage an explosive first two steps forward after the serve. This will allow the server to close in on her first volley and allow less time for the returner to make the passing shot or lob. Players must 'split-step' just before the return is hit to help their balance and movement to the volley. (The timing of this is vital and should be practiced as an important part of volley technique.) The volley should be played with a contact point in front of the body and with a firm wrist on contact with the ball.

DRILL 1.10 **Dominating the Net as a Serving Team**

AIMS
To practice the serve and volley tactic; to establish dominance at the net; to improve communication and highlight individual responsibilities.

LEVEL
Intermediate to advanced

DESCRIPTION
The serving team practices the serve and volley tactic against the coach, who is positioned on the baseline as a returner. The server serves down the middle of the court and follows her serve in to the net. The coach feeds a variety of returns, and the serving team must decide immediately who is to play the volley or smash and where to play it. The server's partner should be encouraged to intercept with a winning volley as much as possible. Targets can be placed on the court to indicate where the first volley should be hit (e.g., down to the feet of the coach's imaginary partner).

COACHING POINTS
The coach should vary the type of returns given as much as possible, combining low balls to the feet with high, floating balls hit down the middle and wide. The coach should also feed down the line if the server's partner moves across too early in anticipation of a middle return. Including the lob down the middle and the lob over the server's partner will fully test the players' communication and organisation. The coach should encourage them to try the I formation and Australian formation when using this drill also. He or she should emphasise good communication, positive movement patterns, and clearly defined roles.

DRILL 1.11 **Developing Accuracy of the Second Serve**

AIMS
To help the server improve the accuracy and variety of direction of her serve; to encourage confidence and commitment when playing this shot.

LEVEL
All

DESCRIPTION
Players play a practice set with the server being allowed only one serve per point. The server is penalised two points if a clean winning return is hit past her but only one point for a serving fault. This difference in scoring should prompt the server to hit with more positive and committed technique, allowing her to develop the shot rather than just being satisfied with serving the ball into court.

DRILL 1.12 **Constructing a Second Serve Pattern by Visualising the Returner's Court Position**

AIMS
To improve serving accuracy; to visualise patterns of play by indicating where the returner is likely to be positioned.

LEVEL
All

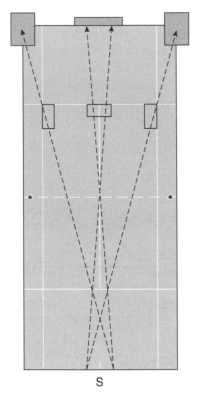

Tactical serving targets placed on the baseline that indicate the returner's court position.

DESCRIPTION
Instead of putting serving targets inside the service box, the coach can place them along the baseline, as shown in the figure, to indicate where the server wants the returner to play the ball from. These targets help the player understand how to construct a second serve pattern because she visualises where the returner is positioned on the court and therefore where her second shot could be played. Using second serve technique only, the player tries to hit 10 serving targets (i.e., she makes the ball travel directly over the baseline target) from 30 attempts. The server should aim for a different target with every serve because this remains realistic to a match situation, in which the server alternates serving sides after each point.

COACHING POINTS
As the serve improves, the target total should be increased. The coach should make a note of which targets the player hits most often to raise her awareness of her favoured serving directions.

DRILL 1.13 Neutralising the Point Using a Second Serve Pattern

AIMS
To learn how to use the direction of the second serve effectively; to develop specific second serve patterns of play.

LEVEL
All

DESCRIPTION
Players play first to seven points with the same player serving until completion. The server is allowed only two shots (including the second serve) to neutralise the point with. Given that the returner will try to dominate off the return, the server must be in at least a neutral (50:50) position in the point after her second shot; otherwise, the ball is stopped and the point lost immediately. Players switch serving and returning roles at the end of the drill.

VARIATION
The point is allowed to continue even if the server hasn't reached a neutral position. If she wins the point, she is awarded one point; if she wins the point *and* reaches neutral after two shots, she is awarded two points instead.

COACHING POINTS
The coach should encourage specific serving patterns. He or she should ask the server what she thinks her opponent's returning strengths are and what type of second shot she wants to hit after serving. The server should judge whether she has recovered to a neutral position, and the returner should judge the same. It is interesting to note each player's perception of the balance of power after a three-shot rally.

DRILL 1.14 Disguising the Direction of the Second Serve

AIMS
To disguise the direction of the serve; to prevent the returner from anticipating the serve's direction.

LEVEL
Intermediate to advanced

DESCRIPTION
The player prepares to serve in the normal way but without deciding the direction of her serve. The coach stands behind the player and instructs her where to serve only *after* she has tossed the ball in the air. This forces the server to hit to different areas of the court using the same ball toss. The drill is completed after the player has hit a total of 10 well-disguised serves.

COACHING POINT
The server should be encouraged to change the action only of her wrist on contact with the ball to vary direction and spin.

DRILL 1.15 Serving With Accuracy and Variety of Direction

AIMS
To emphasise visually the importance of second serve accuracy; to show how important it is to be able to cramp an opponent's returning technique through the body serve.

LEVEL
All

DESCRIPTION
The returner or coach sits on a chair instead of standing in the normal returning position. The server must hit the serve out of her opponent's reach; that is, she must try to make her opponent fall off her chair to hit the return.

VARIATION
Practice the body serve; this ball will be very difficult for the returner to create space for when sitting down.

DRILL 1.16 Moving the Returner Out of Position to Maintain Second Serve Dominance

AIMS
To improve second serve accuracy with the slice or topspin; to disguise the direction of the serve and dictate the playing pattern that follows; to improve tactical awareness by observing how the returner responds to a given serve.

LEVEL
Intermediate to advanced

DESCRIPTION
Players play first to five points with the same player serving until completion. The server is allowed to use only one serve per point, and this serve must make the returner move two steps or more to return the serve. The point is played out only if this is achieved.

VARIATIONS
1. If the returner hasn't moved two steps or more, then the point is stopped immediately and the returner automatically wins the point.
2. The point is allowed to finish even if the returner hasn't moved enough. If the server wins the point, there is no score (i.e., she prevents her opponent from scoring). If the returner wins it, then she scores a point as normal.

COACHING POINTS
The coach should encourage the server to notice which side the returner moves better from and which serve makes her move the most. She should also note whether the slice or topspin second serve forces the returner to move more. Tactical awareness is improved because the server must note her opponent's strengths and weaknesses as well as her own.

DRILL 1.17 Improving Variety of Spin, Direction, and Power When Serving

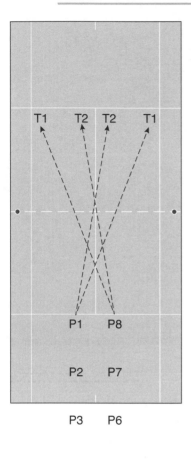

Different serving positions that can be used to help a player increase the feel and strength on her serve.

AIMS
To develop more 'feel' on the serve; to increase its variety of spin and direction; to develop the use of upper- and lower-body strength with serve technique.

LEVEL
All

DESCRIPTION
The player is asked to hit two serves from all eight positions on the court, hitting one wide and one middle serve, until reaching P8. After adequate rest she should repeat the exercise starting from P8 and finishing at P1. The player will hit 32 serves in all.

COACHING POINTS
The coach should encourage more 'feel' by having the player increase the use of the wrist when serving from the short positions (because a loose and flexible wrist will help the ball go in from here). The coach should also encourage more leg drive and upper-body turn when the player is serving from the deep positions (because an increase in lower- and upper-body strength is required to help the ball go in from here).

Tactical Returning

The return of serve is the most important shot in the women's game today. It has become crucial to many players' tactical makeup because of the necessity to counter the threat of the strong server, as well as to dominate the weaker one. A number of different returning tactics are used depending on the intention of the returner, each of which requires specific shot selection, court positioning, and movement.

Many coaches are guilty of not paying enough attention to the return, probably because it is one of the most difficult shots to practice. Unlike the serve, a player requires a playing partner or coach to help her to develop this shot (or a very expensive serving machine!). Coaches often comment on how players find returning practice boring and repetitive (especially if the serve is constantly missed), and on the lack of really effective returning drills. The aim of this chapter is to address these issues by highlighting the key returning tactics used at the highest level and by suggesting a number of ways to develop the return for all levels of players.

The return is a shot that requires particular tactical and technical training. A strong emphasis is placed on a player's receiving skills. Being able to receive the ball in tennis is just as important as being able to send the ball. Receiving skills are more difficult to practice, however, because they are *invisible*; perception and anticipation occur in the player's head before a reaction is seen on the court! However, coaches must help players develop these skills in the same way they help them develop their more visible tennis techniques.

Whether returning the first or second serve, highlighting the three Rs on the return—ready position, reading the ball, and reaction—will help to further improve the execution of this shot. A balanced and alert *ready position* is vital as the returner prepares to face the serve. Key factors include maintaining a still head, relaxed shoulders, a strong posture, flexed knees, and a stable base. The returner should take a small split-step (or 'de-weight') from this ready position as the serve is hit. She should be ready to pick up the flight path of the ball throughout her opponent's service action. Being able to *read* the characteristics of the oncoming ball quickly involves using perception skills. She may be able to pick up clues from her opponent's ball toss, racket action, body positioning, or previous serving habits. She must then try to read the flight path of the serve—its direction, height, depth, speed, and spin—as soon as possible by using her perception of the ball *after* it is hit. The player must *react* with speed and efficiency once she has read the oncoming ball. Turning her upper body immediately toward the direction of the ball, opening her foot stance, and using a simple backswing will help her contact the ball in front of her body—an important ingredient to returning successfully.

Maintaining a low centre of gravity and a stable base will help a player 'win the collision' with the oncoming ball, as well as aid in achieving a swift and balanced recovery position.

This chapter studies the first serve return separately from the second serve return because these two shots usually carry very different tactical objectives. The first serve return is often used to neutralise the threat of a strong first serve, whereas the second serve return is more likely used to create an immediate attacking opportunity. In fact, returning tactics and serving tactics often mirror each other. In other words, first serve return tactics and second serve tactics are often used to neutralise, while second serve return tactics and first serve tactics are often used to attack. With the first serve return, the shot selection of the player remains crucial if she finds herself under pressure from the serve. The options covered in this chapter include the middle return, the inside-out and inside-in return, and the blocked return. With the second serve, the returner can dictate the play by using tactics such as the return and groundstroke attack, return and baseline control, and return and approach. This chapter studies these choices in detail, both in singles and doubles, and suggests a number of drills and practice tips to help make the return an easier shot to improve.

The Neutralising First Serve Return

The first priority for the returner is to neutralise the threat posed by the first serve, thus preventing her opponent from striking first. This means returning well enough so that a neutral position remains after the serve and return have been played. By doing this, the returner may then be able to assert her own authority on the game. This objective is assuming an even greater importance as the length of rally in the women's game continues to shorten. In an interesting study, Peter O'Donoghue and Billy Ingram analysed the average length of rally in women's tennis in 2001. In their study of the four Grand Slams, they found that the average number of shots per rally was 7.0 at the Australian Open, 8.6 at the French Open, 5.8 at Wimbledon, and 6.8 at the US Open (O'Donoghue and Ingram 2001). However, more recent expert opinion suggests that the average length of rally is getting shorter and that in some cases women's rallies are now shorter in length than men's (which averaged 5.2 in 2001 and hasn't significantly changed since). In other words, the returner is having less time and fewer shots to establish an advantage over the server—and the serve and return themselves can count for almost 50 percent of the game!

A player may need to look at the stance, rhythm, and pace of her return, as well as her actual shot selection, to reduce the effectiveness of the first serve. Altering her returning stance can throw a server off her stride because it changes the 'look' that a returner gives her opponent. Taking two steps backward may allow the returner more time to perceive the oncoming ball. Taking two steps forward may intimidate an opponent into 'forcing' the serve too much. Moving more to one side may create a doubt in the server's mind as to the direction she should serve to next.

When players serve extremely well, they usually find themselves sticking to a consistent routine that helps them maintain their rhythm. They take the same amount of time between serves and points, bounce the ball the same number of times, and even try to use the same 'lucky' ball. Breaking this rhythm may require the returner to vary the amount of time she takes between points—for example, 'hustling' the server who likes to play slowly or taking more time against an opponent who likes to play quickly.

Varying the pace of the return may prove effective against an opponent who is constantly dominating with her serve and second shot. Using only blocked returns for a while or 'stepping up to the plate' more often (i.e., hitting more aggressively) can sometimes reduce the server's dominance. It is important to remember that many of these subtle changes in stance, rhythm, or pace don't have to last long. Simply changing one element of the return for a few points can be enough to change the entire feel of a tennis match.

The first serve return tactics covered in this section all involve hitting the return to a high-percentage target, which can be altered as the returner gets used to the style, pace, and shape of the serve. For the more advanced player, this may mean aiming the return toward a relatively small target area that is safely positioned inside the court. This small area allows the returner to narrow her focus onto a specific target while maintaining a high margin for error.

Middle Return

I encourage the middle return hit with quite a flat trajectory straight at the feet of the server. Hitting this 'mirror return' needs a lot of guts, great anticipation, and the skills to effectively cut off the angles when pushed wide.

—Steven Martens, Six-Time Belgium Federation Cup Captain

Returning the first serve down the middle of the court is perhaps the most common returning tactic used on the WTA Tour today. It is a high-percentage shot that allows the returner to play with a large margin for error because it is hit over the lowest part of the net and into the most central part of the court. Crucially, this return allows the player to contact the ball late (always a possibility against a strong first serve) yet still make the shot into the court.

The middle return also reduces the angles available to the server on her second shot. By not giving her an obvious space to hit into, the returner forces the server to decide where to hit to next. The server can easily make an error if she tries to create an angle from this middle position.

Another advantage of the middle return is that it forces the server to move *out of* a space rather than *into* a space. Good footwork and balance are required for moving around the oncoming ball, and many players find this difficult or simply don't practice these movement patterns enough. Tall players, in particular, who use long 'levers' to hit the ball with, can easily become too cramped when trying to hit balls close to their body. In fact, the middle return can cause any server the same problem if hit with enough pace. By contacting the ball in front of the body using a strong, low base and a simple forward swing, the returner can send the serve back so quickly that her opponent has no time to prepare for her next shot. Using the pace of the opponent's shot in this way is highly effective and requires strong, efficient technique and quick perception of the oncoming ball.

To practice the middle return, see drill 2.1 on page 72.

The middle return is also used as a vital tactic in doubles against both the serve and volley player and the player who chooses to serve and stay back. The key here is to prevent the server's partner from intercepting the return at the net. Therefore, the return must be hit with accuracy, because a middle return that floats without purpose will usually be picked off. By making the server play the second shot (whether this is a volley or groundstroke), the players on the returning team buy themselves more time to establish a better court position. They also give themselves a better chance to construct their own winning pattern of play if they neutralise the serving team's position. Conversely, if the server's partner is able to regularly intercept the return, then the returning partners will continually find themselves under pressure, unable to take control of the net or centre of the court.

The middle return may also cause some confusion for a serving team that doesn't have clearly defined roles at the net. This middle ball may tempt both players to go for the volley—or neither of them! This lack of communication will often be experienced by two players playing together for the first time. Their unfamiliarity should be exploited by the returning team whenever possible.

Finally, the middle return can prove highly effective against a serving team that uses the I formation (see chapter 1) and chooses to cover both sides of the court without covering enough of the middle of the court. This situation is often seen with less experienced players at the net who feel the need to move away from the centre of the court to properly cover 'their' half. This can often cause a big gap to appear down the middle for the returner to hit into! The more experienced net player will hold her position in the centre rather than make big moves to either side and will tempt the returner into hitting down her line rather than allowing the middle return. Figure 2.1 illustrates this concept, showing a serving pair playing in an I formation with a first serve hit down the middle from the deuce court. The server follows her serve in to the net and covers the right side of the court, and her partner moves from her central position to cover the left side of the court. This leaves a gap down the middle of the court for the returner to hit her high-percentage return into.

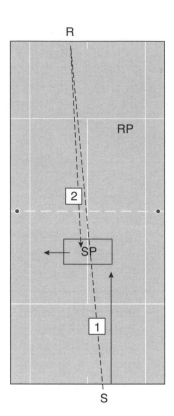

FIGURE 2.1 **Returning against a serving pair that uses the I formation with a serve hit down the middle from the deuce court.**

Inside-Out Return

The inside-out return is another popular shot to play against the serve that is hit down the middle from both the deuce and advantage courts. This shot is hit away from the returner's body (i.e., from 'in' to 'out') and applies equally to right- and left-handers playing both forehands and backhands. The forehand inside-out return is a well-established shot. The backhand inside-out return has evolved more recently because the speed of the first serve now prevents many players from running around their backhand side to hit the forehand return. As a result, players have been forced to hit backhands across the court instead, developing the backhand inside-out return into a recognised weapon.

The inside-out return can be used most effectively against the server who struggles to move quickly enough to the wide ball from the finishing position of her serve, or who lacks reach (for example, a player who uses two hands on both sides). It can also be used in combination with the sneak approach because sometimes the inside-out return can force the server into a defensive position (because of the angle of the return) immediately. This allows the returner to capitalise by finishing the point with a volley or short groundstroke if the server has been put under enough pressure.

This return carries a high margin of error because the ball is hit across the court (into the longest part of the court) into a large target area. It also allows the returner to send the ball back in the same direction of the serve. This is an important point because trying to change the direction of a ball travelling up to 192 km/h (120 mph) can be difficult! As with the middle return, if the inside-out return is caught late, then the player still has a good chance of playing an effective shot into court. Figure 2.2 shows the target area for the inside-out return played from the deuce court. In this figure, a right-handed returner has hit her inside-out backhand return across the court against a first serve hit down the middle from the deuce court. Note how this shot is hit into a high-percentage target, allowing plenty of scope for a mistimed return to remain effective. The same target would be used for the left-handed returner hitting her inside-out forehand.

To practice inside-out returns, see drill 2.2 on page 73.

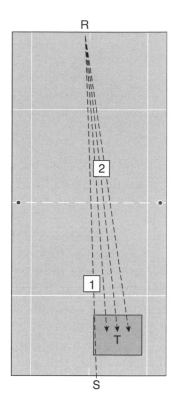

FIGURE 2.2 Target area for the inside-out return hit from the deuce court.

The inside-out return is also an important shot to develop for the returning team in doubles because it steers the ball away from the server's partner at the net. A key factor in breaking serve in doubles is to make the server play as many second shots as possible from a first serve situation. The inside-out return helps the returning team do this. This shot can be used to great effect against the serve and volleyer because a well-timed return hit short and wide of the incoming server will force her to hit a low volley from a wide position. This will give the returner's partner a chance to intercept with a winning volley of her own.

A serving team may counteract the threat of a strong inside-out return by using an Australian formation. The server's partner will stand at the net on the same side of the court as the server—directly in the line of the inside-out return. In this case, the returner may choose to use the *inside-in* return or the inside-out lob instead. The returning team should be careful, however, when using this return against a serving team using the I formation. This is because the server's partner often moves across the court from her middle position at the net—directly into the path of the inside-out return! (For more information about the Australian and I formations, please see chapter 1.)

Inside-In Return

The inside-in return, hit down the line (as opposed to the inside-out return, which is hit across the court), is another recognised shot that is played against the middle serve from either the forehand or backhand side. Although this shot is a lower-percentage one because it is hit over the higher part of the net and into a shorter length of court, it still provides the returner with a large margin of error in terms of target area. This is because a late return hit across the body will drift farther inside the court. This contrasts sharply with a return hit down the line from a wide serve, where the ball, if caught late, will drift farther outside the court.

Figures 2.3 and 2.4 demonstrate this crucial difference in margins between a down-the-line return hit from a middle serve and a wide serve. In figure 2.3 this right-handed returner has hit a backhand down the line against a serve hit down the middle from the deuce court. This shot, hit across the body, carries a high margin of error because a late return will drift farther inside the court. In figure 2.4 the same right-handed returner has hit a forehand down the line against a serve

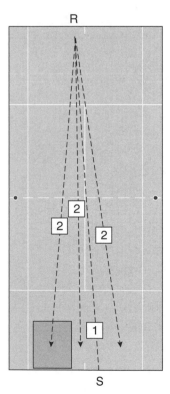

FIGURE 2.3 The inside-in return hit against the middle serve from the deuce court.

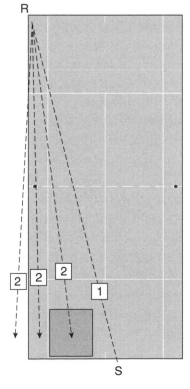

FIGURE 2.4 The down-the-line return hit against the wide serve from the deuce court.

hit out wide from the deuce court. This time, any type of late return will drift farther outside the court.

The inside-in return gives a player the chance to manoeuvre her opponent away from the centre of the court. The key to its success lies in the returner's court position because the wider the position on the court the returner plays from, the more exposed she becomes to her opponent's second shot into the space. Therefore, this return must be played from a fairly central court position. In figure 2.5, a strong first serve is hit into the body of this right-handed returner from the deuce court. She chooses to hit the backhand inside-in return down the line. With her body weight moving out of the court, she has created a big space for the server to hit her second shot into. From this position, the returner would be better off playing the backhand inside-out return, which at least forces the server to hit her second shot into the space down the line—a lower-percentage shot that she may be less comfortable executing. The inside-in return, therefore, is hit more effectively from a central court position (see figure 2.6) because the net is lower and there is more space to hit into. The returner

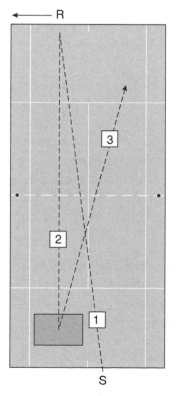
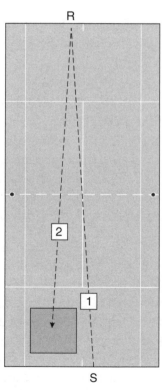
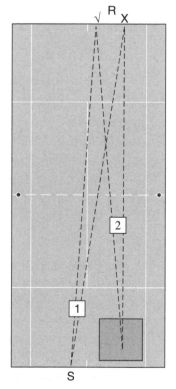

FIGURE 2.5 The backhand inside-in return hit against the body serve hit from the deuce court.

FIGURE 2.6 The backhand inside-in return hit against the middle serve hit from the deuce court.

FIGURE 2.7 The forehand inside-in return hit down the line from the advantage court.

maintains a more central court position because the serve has been hit straight down the middle of the court, preventing her from having to move toward the sideline to hit her backhand. As a result, less space is created for the server to hit her second shot into. The inside-in return hit from the forehand side, shown on the previous page in figure 2.7, is also used more effectively from a central position for the same reasons.

To practice the tactics discussed in this section, see drill 2.3 on page 74.

The inside-in return is not used often in doubles because, as mentioned before, the primary aim of the returning team is to make the server play as many second shots as possible. In other words, the crosscourt (inside-out) return is used far more often than the down-the-line (inside-in) return against a first serve. However, it should be used as a surprise tactic on occasion, as well as against a net player who moves across the net too early when trying to intercept. It can also be used effectively against a particularly weak net player (in the same way that the serve and groundstroke attack tactic is used; see chapter 1).

Blocked Return

Using the blocked return is another common way of defending against the strong first serve. This shot requires the returner to absorb the pace of the serve by using a short swing and by contacting the ball in front of her body with a firm wrist, similar to a volley technique. This short swing gives her a better chance of timing the ball correctly and, therefore, hitting to a more accurate target on court. Also, the slower pace of the blocked return gives her more time to recover to a central court position.

The blocked return can be used effectively in three main tactical scenarios:

1. Against an opponent who dislikes the slower pace and bounce of a blocked return. This is becoming an increasingly relevant tactic in the women's game today because most players are now comfortable playing against the fast, flat ball. Because opportunities to play against the slow ball are fewer, the blocked return can now be used as a weapon! The counterpuncher, in particular, who uses the pace of her opponent's ball to attack with, may become frustrated at having to generate her own pace against this shot. In a similar way, hitting the blocked return to a short, wide target may force the server to move in to the net against her wishes—allowing the returner to hit

an aggressive passing shot or lob as her second shot (this tactic is illustrated in drill 2.4). Being able to reduce as well as increase the pace of the oncoming ball is a key skill to acquire for tennis.

2. When the returner needs a high percentage of returns in court. Very often during a match the returner simply needs to make her opponent play in order to put pressure on her. This could be when the server is struggling with nerves, anger, fatigue, or injury, for example. Using the blocked return in these situations will force the server to hit more balls and to concentrate for longer periods of time.

3. When the serve puts the returner under extreme pressure. The blocked return is often played against a strong and accurate first serve, especially with a wide serve that threatens to drag the returner completely out of court. The aim here is to play the return as deep and as centrally as possible, giving the server little space or angle to use for her second shot. This tactic is particularly relevant against an opponent who relies on hitting a lot of unreturnable serves. Making her work harder for her service games could make the difference between winning and losing a close match.

To practice the blocked return, see drill 2.4 on page 75.

The blocked return is a very common tactical tool used in doubles. The simpler technique used to play the block allows for a greater degree of control, enabling the returner to play to more specific areas of the court. (This is important in doubles because there is less space on the court.) In general, the blocked return has three main tactical uses.

The first use is against the serve and volley player. The aim of the returner is to block the return down to the feet of the oncoming server, forcing her to play her first volley (or half volley) up and over the net from a low position. This provides the returner's partner with an excellent opportunity to intercept with a winning volley or may allow the returner to approach the net herself if the server is under extreme pressure. The blocked return is ideal to use in this situation because control rather than pace is the key to this tactic's success.

The second use is as a lob, either over the server's partner or down the middle of the court. This shot is often seen in women's doubles and is typically played against a strong, wide serve. The lob over the server's partner forces the serving team to change its court positioning. It is especially effective when played against the serve and volley player, who has to change direction and quickly cover the area behind her partner. The lob down the middle allows the returning team time to regain a stronger court position, and may allow the returner the chance to approach the net if the server stays back.

The third use is when the serve puts the returner under extreme pressure. As in singles, this shot may give the returner the only realistic chance of making the ball in the court. In doubles, if the return is weak, the returner's partner must quickly readjust her position by moving backward. This gives her and her partner the best chance of defending against the serving team's aggressive second shot.

Coaching Tip

The return of serve is probably the most underpracticed shot in the game. Returning practice often becomes too static if the server keeps missing the serve! Also, it is difficult for the coach to serve to the player and watch her returning technique at virtually the same time. Coaches, therefore, need to work hard at engaging their players when developing this shot. For example:

1. The player could be given the chance to play out the point after her third effective return in a row.

2. Players could play a set using only the serve and return. The server wins the point if the return is missed, whereas the returner wins the point if she makes the return. Specific serve and return targets could be used to increase or decrease the difficulty of the task for each player.

3. Coaches could serve from inside the baseline to improve the consistency and accuracy of their feed, and to allow a closer look at the player's returning technique.

4. Coaches could feed the player alternate serves and groundstrokes. This will give her the chance to feel the difference in technique between a normal groundstroke and a return (e.g., using a shorter swing on the return).

Returning the Left-Handed Serve

The left-handed first serve will often cause the right-handed returner problems because its movement is less familiar. This means that the slice serve (the most common serve in women's tennis) will naturally move to the returner's backhand side rather than forehand side. This 'turn' on the ball makes it very difficult for the right-hander to run around her backhand side to attack with the forehand. In many cases the returner will be better off letting the ball come to the backhand rather than getting caught up trying to create space for the forehand—especially when returning the first serve.

The wide serve hit from the advantage court, in particular, can be difficult to neutralise. Not only does the movement of the serve take the returner out of the court, but the natural instinct to return crosscourt (having a high margin of error) may also play into the lefty's hands! This is because the crosscourt return allows the server to hit her forehand down the line into the space that has been created. Many left-handers enjoy hitting this type of forehand because they have spent years rallying crosscourt against the right-hander's backhand and are used to moving to this side. Figure 2.8 shows how this serve can open up the court for the left-hander.

A more effective alternative can be to hit down the middle of the court against the wide first serve from the advantage court. With this return the server is no longer given a natural space to hit into; instead she has to create a space with fewer angles available to her. Also, she now has to move around the ball instead of moving to the ball—a movement pattern that she may not be comfortable using.

In figure 2.9 the left-handed server hits the same wide first serve from the advantage court. This time, the returner hits directly down the middle of the court rather than crosscourt, forcing the server to move out of the way of the ball. This middle target reduces the angles available to the server and gives the returner a better chance of neutralising the server's dominance.

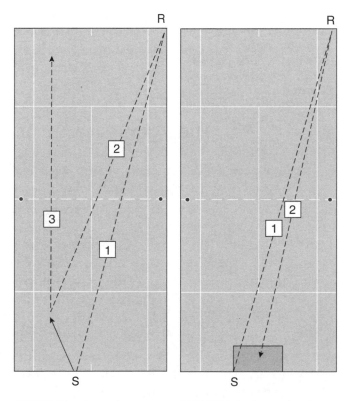

FIGURE 2.8 Returning crosscourt against the left-handed first serve hit out wide from the advantage court.

FIGURE 2.9 Returning down the middle against the left-handed first serve hit out wide from the advantage court.

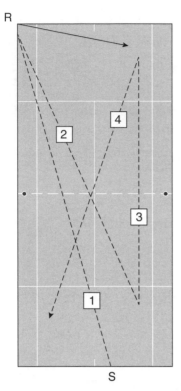

FIGURE 2.10 Using the left-handed crosscourt return against the wide serve hit from the deuce court.

Left-Handed Return

The right-handed server will often try to expose the left-handed returner by hitting her first serve out wide from the deuce court. The server will try to pull the returner out of the court using a slice serve that naturally moves to the backhand side. However, returning the backhand crosscourt from this position can often prove more effective because many right-handers prefer to move around the ball when hitting aggressive forehands rather than move to the ball (as opposed to the left-hander's preference).

In this situation, left-handed returners with a strong running forehand often lure their opponents into a counterpunching trap when receiving the wide serve to the backhand from the deuce court. By returning crosscourt, the returner tempts the server to hit her second shot down the line into the space. This pattern sets up the returner's favourite running forehand to hit as her second shot! Figure 2.10 shows how this pattern works.

The Aggressive Second Serve Return

Waiting for the kill is extinct now. Now you have to take advantage of every ball you have.

—Nick Bollettieri, tennis coach whose tennis academy has helped develop nine World Number 1 players

Statistics prove that the female server will generally lose more than half of the second serve points she plays. Table 2.1 illustrates that at Wimbledon, from 2000 to 2006, the server continually won far fewer than 50 percent of her second serve points. Indeed, in all four Grand Slams of 2006, the server was shown to win an average of only 41 percent. These figures clearly show that the second serve return represents an excellent opportunity for the returner to dominate the server immediately. She simply cannot afford to miss the chance to attack if the serve is weak because this may be her only guaranteed short ball of the rally! She should view this shot in the same way as she views her own first serve—as a chance

Table 2.1 Percentage of Second Serve Points Won in Women's Singles at Wimbledon

Year	1st Round	2nd Round	3rd Round	4th Round	Q/Final	S/Final	Final	Total
2000	45	46	48	45	43	35	35	42%
2001	45	46	44	47	36	44	43	44%
2002	45	46	43	48	50	50	45	47%
2003	44	47	46	42	44	41	34	43%
2004	46	47	41	43	49	45	52	46%
2005	39	39	40	39	44	43	41	41%
2006	41	41	40	37	39	36	56	41%

Based on statistics from the IBM Wimbledon Information System, courtesy of IBM

to act rather than react. Of the four possible ways to start a rally, these two shots represent the best chance to attack.

Because not many female players vary their serve's spin, pace, or direction, it is very common to see the same type of second serve being hit throughout a match. This allows the returner to quickly get used to how the serve moves and where it goes. Her ability to anticipate the serve early in a match means that the returner can start to use her return as the first shot in one of the aggressive patterns of play outlined in the coming sections.

Return and Groundstroke Attack

I love to see the girls pressure the second serve by using early, aggressive groundstrokes hit down the line.

—Amy Jensen, Three-Time NCAA Doubles Champion

The return and groundstroke attack is often used against a weak second serve hit out wide from either side that creates a natural space for the returner to hit into. The returner hits the return aggressively, either crosscourt or down the line, from inside the baseline, allowing the server very little time to recover from her serving position. The returner maintains control of the court by hitting an aggressive second shot, also from inside the baseline, into the opposite space she hit the first return into, increasing the time pressure on her opponent. This lack of time is the key to this tactic's success, which explains why many second shot winners are hit well within the lines. The server simply cannot reach the ball in time. To execute this tactic well, a player must be able to return the serve and hit her second shot from on or inside the baseline, usually hitting the ball at, or just after, the top of its bounce. Many players on the WTA Tour are now deliberately returning aggressively to the *forehand* side of the server more often than the backhand side. This is because the server will usually have to move her grip more to hit a forehand after serving than to hit a backhand.

Figures 2.11 and 2.12 show how the returner can powerfully combine her first two shots against the wide second serve. In figure 2.11 a second serve has been hit out wide from the deuce court. The returner hits an aggressive crosscourt return, which forces the server to hit down the line under pressure (her contact point is too late to be able to hit crosscourt). The returner then hits her second shot crosscourt into the opposite space that has been created. Note how both the return and second shot have been hit from inside the baseline. The returner could hit her return down the line from this serve instead. In this case she would maintain her dominance by hitting her second shot into the opposite space again, either crosscourt or down the line, depending on where the server's second shot has been played. In figure 2.12 the returner has hit down the line against the second serve hit wide from the deuce court. This time the server has been able to defend crosscourt, so the returner hits her second shot down the line into the opposite space. Again, the returner's second shot is hit from well inside the baseline. The same patterns can also be played against the wide serve hit from the advantage court.

When returning second serves that are hit down the middle from either the deuce or advantage court, play-

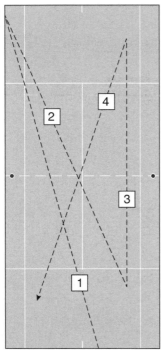

FIGURE 2.11 Hitting the crosscourt return against the wide second serve hit from the deuce court.

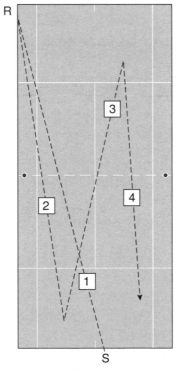

FIGURE 2.12 The down-the-line return played against the wide second serve hit from the deuce court.

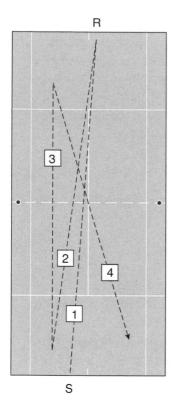

FIGURE 2.13 **The middle return played against a second serve hit down the middle from the advantage court.**

ers have fewer angles to work with. As a result, an aggressive middle return can be used to set up an opening for the returner's second shot. This middle return is hit with just as much aggression and with the same early court position, but is hit right back at the server. The returner's goal is to put the server under so much time and pace pressure that an error is forced or a space is opened up for the second shot. Figure 2.13 illustrates this tactic. A similar pattern could also develop from the deuce court.

Using the return and groundstroke attack early in a match can strongly influence the way an opponent plays and feels. It gives the returner the chance to dominate tactically by exerting time and pace pressure. These two forms of pressure may force an opponent to take some pace off her first serve to prevent the returner from facing many second serves. (If this happens, there is no reason the returner shouldn't pressure the first serve in the same way as well!) It also gives the returner the chance to threaten psychologically by taking up an intimidating playing position on or inside the baseline. This is an important point because the returning stance is perhaps the most noticeable position a player will take up during a match; the server literally looks directly at the returner before serving.

To practice returning from an aggressive court position, see drill 2.5 on page 76.

In doubles, this aggressive groundstroke return, hit from inside the baseline, is often played down the line—straight at the server's partner. Figure 2.14 shows how the returning team can take control of the court by returning down the line against the second serve hit wide from the advantage court. This tactic is used from both sides of the court and is most effective when played as the returner's first or second shot of

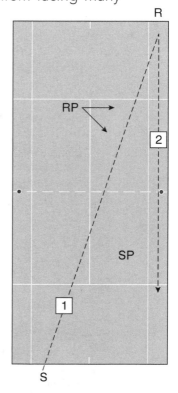

FIGURE 2.14 **The aggressive return hit down the line against the wide serve from the advantage court in doubles.**

the rally because it prevents the serving team from settling into a rhythm. It is used in particular against a server whose strength lies in hitting crosscourt groundstrokes and also against a server's partner who has a weak volley. The returner's partner must know in advance that the returner is going to hit down the line because this will allow her to cover the middle part of the court in anticipation of a defensive volley. The returner continues to attack with aggressive groundstrokes hit either crosscourt or down the line until she forces an error or her partner can intercept with a winning volley.

To practice the tactics discussed in this section, see drill 2.6 on page 77.

Return and Baseline Control

Often during a match the returner will want to maintain her dominance over the server without having a planned shot to hit after an aggressive return—usually when the opponent has defended deep down the middle of the court. Instead, she will try to prevent the server from regaining a neutral position by hitting a sequence of dominating shots that continually increase the pressure on her opponent. She will look to finish the point only after a short ball or after a natural space has opened up.

© Icon Sports Media

Dominating with the second serve return is a crucial tactic in women's tennis.

This patient yet aggressive approach should be encouraged because players often make the mistake of trying to continually hit winning returns when they don't need to. They can become scared of losing control of the point if the ball comes back too often. Experienced players who maintain control of the point successfully are prepared to hit a number of shots, if necessary, before winning the point. They simply try to make their opponent defend for as long as possible rather than try to hit any outright winning shots. This difference in mentality is crucial because, for these players, the second serve return becomes the first shot in a winning sequence rather than the only shot!

This tactic is particularly relevant for the younger player who doesn't hit with much power. In this case, she will often play the return with a number of groundstrokes to create an advantage, while maintaining the long-term goal of using the return and groundstroke attack tactic as she develops more weight of shot.

To practice maintaining baseline control after the return, see drill 2.7 on page 78.

The same baseline control tactic is used by the returning team in doubles, especially for those returners who prefer playing aggressively from the baseline rather than coming in to the net. In this case, the returner will choose to play crosscourt more often to build pressure through a series of aggressive groundstrokes. Her partner at the net will continually look for an opportunity to win the point with an intercept volley. Again, the better the crosscourt groundstroke is, the more chance the returner's partner has of finishing the point from the net.

Figure 2.15 shows the return and baseline control tactic being used in doubles against the second serve hit down the middle from the deuce court. The serve is followed by a series of crosscourt groundstrokes between the server and returner. Once the returner gains control of the rally, her partner looks to intercept with a winning volley into the shaded target area. Note how the volley target area is positioned in the middle of the court and how the returner's partner moves forward to her intercept volley.

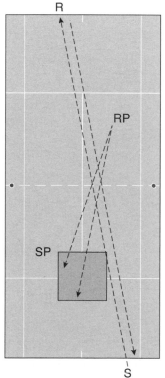

FIGURE 2.15 The return and baseline control tactic used against the second serve hit down the middle from the deuce court.

Return and Drive Volley

The return and drive volley is an exciting tactic that has recently been established in the women's game. Instead of allowing this ball to bounce, and possibly losing her dominant position, the returner instinctively chooses to play this shot out of the air as a drive volley. An early, aggressively hit second serve return can often force a high, defensive reply from the server. As with the groundstroke attack tactics mentioned earlier, the amount of time and pace pressure exerted on the server is the key to this tactic's success.

Figures 2.16 and 2.17 show how the drive volley can be hit either into the space (figure 2.16) or back behind the server (figure 2.17) depending on how quickly the opponent is able to recover. In figure 2.16 a second serve is hit out wide from the advantage court. A powerful return hit from inside the baseline has forced the server to defend with a high shot hit down the line. The returner has recognised this ball as a drive volley and moves farther inside the court to play it out of the air. She hits crosscourt into the space that has been created. Note that only a large target area is needed for the drive volley because time pressure, rather than accuracy, often wins the returner the point. In figure 2.17 the same aggressive return has been hit forcing the high, defensive shot hit down the line. This time the returner sees the server recovering too quickly across the court, so she hits her drive volley down the line—back behind her opponent. Again, the same large target area is used for her drive volley.

It is also important for the returner to notice which side of her opponent elicits a higher, more defensive return. For example, an aggressive return hit wide

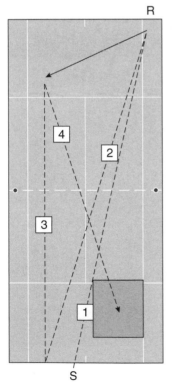

FIGURE 2.16   The drive volley hit into the space, being used as part of the return and drive volley tactic.

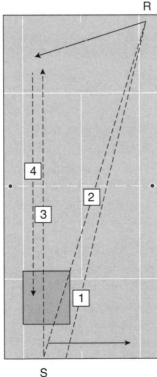

FIGURE 2.17   The drive volley hit back behind the server, being used as part of the return and drive volley tactic.

to a single-handed backhand may force more high balls than the same return hit to the double-handed backhand. This is because the single-hander may be forced to hit a slice backhand that may float because of a lack of strength when played under extreme pressure.

To practice using the drive volley after the return, see drill 2.8 on page 79.

The drive volley will be used as a second shot by the returning team in doubles just as it is in singles. In other words, a dominating second serve return will often be followed by a drive volley that is hit either crosscourt to the server or down the line to the server's partner at the net. This is similar to how the return and ground-stroke attack is used. Again, this tactic allows the returning team to maintain control of the court by applying time and pace pressure onto their opponents. Players who lack confidence in their normal volley technique should choose to use this tactic whenever possible (because the drive volley is similar to groundstroke technique in its execution).

Return and Sneak

Using the return and sneak tactic is another way of applying pressure on an opponent by not giving her enough time to recover from her serving position. In this situation the returner hits an aggressive return and then looks for the opportunity to 'sneak' in to the net. The sneak, like the drive volley, is an instinctive movement based on the amount of pressure an opponent is under. When using this tactic, the returner naturally moves forward, inside the baseline, before deciding whether her opponent is under enough pressure. This holding position allows her the option of coming in to the net or returning to the baseline, depending on the strength of her opponent's next shot. Players decide to sneak based on the time, pace, and positional pressure exerted on their opponent. This tactic could be used most effectively against the player who blocks the ball when under pressure. This slower-moving ball often gives the returner the chance to sneak close enough in to the net so she can hit an attacking volley. Figure 2.18

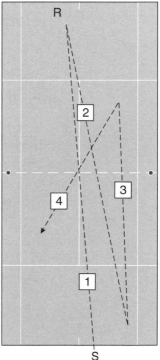

FIGURE 2.18 Using the return and sneak tactic against a second serve hit down the middle from the deuce court.

shows how an aggressive second serve return, hit across the court against a middle serve from the deuce court, can create a sneak opportunity. In this figure, the return has forced the server to defend with a weak second shot, hit late and down the line. The returner, seeing her opponent under pressure, instinctively sneaks in to the net to meet her opponent's second shot with a short angle volley.

To practice the return and sneak tactic, see drill 2.9 on page 80.

This tactic is similar to the return and drive volley tactic in that both require the player to make instinctive decisions rather than planned ones. This is also the case for the returning player in doubles, who sees an opportunity to move in to the net if the server is playing too defensively. If the server's second shot floats wide of the returner's partner at the net, the returner should instinctively move in and volley this ball herself. This tactic may force the server into taking more risks by playing more aggressively to counter this threat—and making more errors in the process as a result. If the returner is to use this tactic frequently, she should consciously take up a position just inside the baseline after hitting her return. This position allows her easy access to the net if she wishes.

Return and Planned Approach

Using the return as an approach can be used as a planned tactic as well as an instinctive one. This means that the returner commits herself to approaching the net with her return, regardless of how effective her opponent's serve and her own return is—making it a slightly more risky tactic. This differs from the instinctual approach, in which the returner gives herself the chance to see the effectiveness of her return before approaching. The planned approach, however, usually gives the player the chance to close in tighter on the net because she doesn't wait to see the outcome of her return—she just goes for it! This closer positioning to the net reduces the space available for the opponent to hit her passing shot into.

As a rule, the return and planned approach tactic is used less frequently today because so many players enjoy having a net target to pass or lob against. However, there are still two main scenarios in which this tactic can work: the 'chip and charge' and the drive-in.

In the chip and charge tactic, a player returns with slice (chip) and immediately follows in to the net (charge). The chip and charge was made famous by such greats as Martina Navratilova and Billie Jean King, who regularly approached the net behind a sliced backhand (and sometimes forehand) return. The short, simple technique used to slice the return allows the player to control the oncoming ball. The slice itself keeps the ball low to the ground, making it difficult to attack and forcing the opponent to hit up over the net. For these reasons, players such as Justine Henin-Hardenne and Amelie Mauresmo, who possess excellent slice backhands, will sometimes approach the net behind either a short crosscourt, or a deep-down-the-line or middle return.

Figures 2.19 and 2.20 show how these two backhand returns can prove effective from both the deuce and advantage courts. Figure 2.19 shows a right-handed returner using her backhand slice to approach the net against a second serve hit down the middle from the deuce court. Note how this shot can either be hit down the line or down the middle of the court, allowing the server no obvious space to hit into. Figure 2.20 shows a right-handed returner using the same backhand slice to approach the net against the serve hit wide from the advantage court. This serve gives the returner more angles to work with so she can play either the down-the-line approach or the short angle, crosscourt approach. Note how the short angle approach can effectively drag the server up the court and force her to hit high over the net (because the slice stays so low).

Players using the backhand slice could also approach the net with the drop shot return as an alternative. They are able to disguise this shot until the very last moment because the shot preparation looks almost the same as the backhand slice. In this situation, the direction of the drop shot (i.e., down the line, middle, or crosscourt) is less important than its disguise; the surprise factor usually beats the server. The player will approach the net after playing the drop shot return because

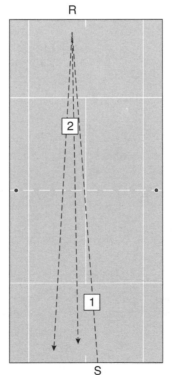

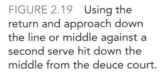

FIGURE 2.19 Using the return and approach down the line or middle against a second serve hit down the middle from the deuce court.

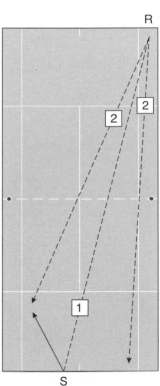

FIGURE 2.20 Using the return and approach down the line or short crosscourt against a second serve hit out wide from the advantage court.

the server is likely to be scrambling for the ball—probably hitting high and short if under pressure. This becomes an easy ball for the returner to volley against.

In the drive-in tactic, players use the topspin return (the drive) to approach the net with. Again, this planned approach requires the player to return the ball and approach the net regardless of how good her return actually is. The key difference between this tactic and the chip and charge tactic is that the ball is hit with topspin rather than slice. This means that the ball will bounce higher but can be hit with more pace also. Therefore, to be truly effective, the drive-in must put the server under time and pace pressure. This tactic should be used against a server who continually defends with a high or blocked second shot (because this ball should be easy to volley against). This can be used potently when played as a surprise tactic on certain big points. By approaching the net, the returner forces her opponent to hit a winning shot immediately. This may unnerve the server enough to force her into error.

To practice the return and planned approach tactic, see drill 2.10 on page 81.

The return and planned approach is more commonly used in doubles because it gives the returning team the chance to control the net. This is a key tactic in doubles. The best doubles players in the world will approach the net with both the chip and charge and drive-in returns as often as possible. Because of the lack of space on the doubles court compared to the singles court, players must hit these returns to very specific areas of the court against both the server who stays back and the server who uses the serve and volley tactic.

Against the server who stays back, the returner plays deep crosscourt (away from the server's partner at the net) and follows in to join her partner at the net. This return will often be hit using the slice from either the forehand or backhand side. The slice return usually travels slower through the air than the topspin return, and this allows the player more time to take up a better net position. When the returner hits with topspin she may find that the ball comes back too quickly. In this situation the returner will have less time to come in because the ball reaches the server more quickly (because it is travelling faster) and therefore is hit back to her more quickly! Also, a good slice return will stay lower than the topspin return and will force the opponent to hit the ball higher over the net, making it easier to volley.

Against the server who uses the serve and volley tactic, the return needs to be hit short crosscourt (away from the server's partner again), down to the feet of the oncoming volleyer. This type of return forces the server to hit her volley high over the net from a short and low position, allowing the returner the chance to move in and dominate the point with an aggressive volley. It can also give her partner an opportunity to intercept with a winning volley, hit either down the middle of the court or straight at one of her opponents.

Hitting the lob return is another option for the player wishing to approach the net immediately. This is hit down the line with either slice or topspin, over the head of the server's partner.

This shot is very effective against the serve and volley player because it forces the server to cover the area behind her partner—an area that she is swiftly moving away from as she approaches the net. The lob allows the returner plenty of time to approach with and also forces the serving team to change its formation (the server's partner has to switch sides because her partner will be hitting the next shot from directly behind her). The lob can also be used against the server who stays back, although it may not put the serving team under quite so much pressure given that the server is already positioned on the baseline. However, it still allows the returning team to take control of the net and forces the serving team to change its formation.

Figure 2.21 shows a second serve hit out wide from the advantage court. As the server follows in behind it, the returner hits the lob over the server's partner. Note how the server has to change direction (from moving toward the net to moving away from

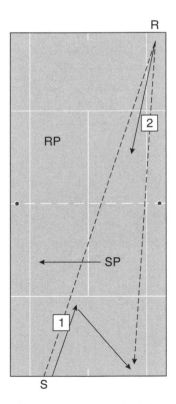

FIGURE 2.21 Using the lob return and approach against the serve and volleyer in doubles.

the net) and cover the area behind her partner. Note also how her partner has to switch sides to cover the other side of the court. The returner simply follows her lob in to the net to join her partner.

Whichever tactic is used, the returner's partner must know the tactical intention of the returner in *advance* so she can anticipate the opponent's possible responses ahead of time and position herself accordingly. For example, if she knows that her partner will hit the lob return, she can prepare to move in closer to the net if the lob is successful, or move away from the net if the lob is short. Therefore, constant communication between the returner and her partner is vital, not only between points and games but during points as well.

To practice the return and planned approach in doubles, see drill 2.11 on page 82.

Returning Percentages

The effectiveness of the return can be measured like that of the serve. Doing so will provide valuable feedback to both player and coach. By analysing her performance in this way, the player can set more realistic and specific goals for her return of serve in the future. For example, the statistics may show that a player wins twice as many points returning with her backhand than with her forehand. In this case, she will clearly work to improve her forehand return—and the tactics she uses alongside it. Figure 2.22 is a returning summary. To calculate the various percentage statistics that help indicate a player's returning performance, divide the first number in the sequence by the second number and multiply by 100.

Summary

☐ To return effectively, a player needs to assume a balanced and alert *ready* position, she must *read* the flight path of the oncoming ball quickly, and she must *react* with speed and efficiency.

☐ The first priority for the returner is to neutralise the threat posed by the first serve. This means returning well enough so that a neutral position remains after the serve and return have been played.

Returning Summary

_____ (number of first serve returns in) / _____ (number of first serve return attempts)

= _____ percentage of first serve returns in

_____ (number of second serve returns in) / _____ (number of second serve return attempts)

= _____ percentage of second serve returns in

_____ (number of first serve return points won) / _____ (total number of first serve return points)

= _____ percentage of first serve return points won

_____ (number of second serve return points won) / _____ (total number of second serve return points)

= _____ percentage of second serve return points won

_____ (number of points won when returning with forehand, backhand) / _____ (total number of points returned with forehand, backhand)

= _____ percentage of forehand, backhand returns won

_____ (number of unreturnable returns) / _____ (total number of returning points)

= _____ percentage of unreturnable returns

FIGURE 2.22   **Returning summary.**

☐ The return down the middle provides a high-percentage option in singles and doubles because it is hit over the lowest part of the net and into the most central part of the court. It also prevents the server from using any natural angle for her second shot. The middle return is hit straight back at the server, forcing her to move out of a space rather than into a space. It is used very effectively against tall, long-limbed opponents.

☐ The inside-out return is a popular shot to play against the serve that is hit down the middle, from both the deuce and advantage courts. This shot is hit away from the returner's body (i.e., from 'in' to 'out') and applies equally to right- and left-handers playing both forehands and backhands. Again, it carries a high margin of error because the return is hit across the court (into the longest part of the court) and without the player needing to change the direction of the ball since it is hit back in the direction of the serve.

☐ The inside-in return, hit down the line, is another recognised shot that is played against the middle serve. This return carries a higher risk because it is hit over the higher part of the net and into a shorter length of court, although it still provides the returner with a large margin of error in terms of target area. It is more effective when hit from a central court position because it is easier to recover back to the middle of the court from here. It is occasionally used in doubles when the returner wants to hit down the line (especially if she sees the opposing net player move across the net too early).

☐ A player will use the blocked return if she deliberately wants to slow the pace of the ball down, if she needs a high percentage of returns in court, or if the serve puts her under extreme pressure. In doubles, the blocked return can be used effectively against the serve and volleyer (to hit down to the server's feet), as a lob (either over the server's partner or down the middle of the court), or when under extreme pressure from the serve.

☐ The left-handed serve will often cause the right-handed returner problems because its movement is less familiar. This means that the slice serve (the most common serve in women's tennis) will naturally move to the returner's backhand side rather than forehand side. It is natural for her to want to return crosscourt from here, but this may suit the left-handed player who hits a strong forehand down the line. Returning down the middle of the court may prove a better option.

☐ The left-handed returner will face the same situation when returning the wide serve hit from the deuce court.

☐ Statistics prove that the majority of second serve points are won by the returner; therefore, the second serve return represents an excellent opportunity for a player to dictate the point immediately.

☐ The return and groundstroke attack tactic involves the return being hit aggressively and from inside the baseline; the returner maintains control of the court by hitting an aggressive second shot, also from inside the baseline. This increases the time pressure on her opponent. In doubles, this aggressive return is often played down the line—straight at the server's partner.

☐ A player will use the return and baseline control tactic when she has no obvious planned second shot to hit. She will try to prevent the server from regaining a neutral position by hitting a sequence of dominating shots that continually increase the pressure on her opponent. The same approach is used by the returning team in doubles; the returner will look to control a crosscourt baseline rally so her partner can try to win the point with an intercept volley at the net.

☐ The return and drive volley, and the return and sneak tactics both involve the returner making an instinctive decision to play a volley after an aggressive return. The drive volley will usually be hit against the high, floating ball, whereas the sneak volley will be hit against the lower one. Both of these tactics apply equally to singles and doubles play.

☐ Approaching the net behind the return can be used as a planned tactic also. A player may choose to approach with a slice return (chip and charge) or with an aggressive topspin return (drive-in). Both approaches are used often in doubles; the slice return sometimes is hit deep crosscourt (against the server who stays back), short crosscourt (against the serve and volleyer), or as a lob over the server's partner.

☐ The effectiveness of the return can be measured in the same way as that of the serve. This research provides valuable feedback to both coach and player.

DRILL 2.1   Developing the Middle Return

AIMS
To develop the middle return; to neutralise the threat of the strong first serve.

LEVEL
All

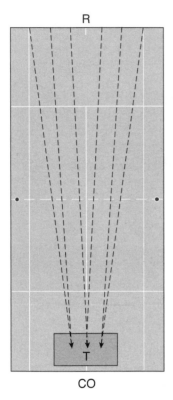

The target area used for the middle return.

DESCRIPTION
The coach (or practice partner) serves a variety of first serves to a player who must return down the middle of the court into the target area. The player keeps score as to how many returns are able to neutralise the threat of the serve (through a combination of accuracy, pace, and spin). If there are two players, they should switch serving and returning roles frequently because asking one player to continually hit first serves will cause injury.

VARIATION
The server or returner judges whether the return is good enough to neutralise. This will increase each player's general tactical awareness. The target should stay on the court during points play (using nonslip markers), and the point should continue only if the return lands inside the target area.

COACHING POINTS
The coach should point out the returning side the player hits from most effectively and whether she hits this return from a middle, body, or wide serve. This will help her to understand which types of return need further improvement and which ones she should look to use regularly in a match. The coach should also watch how quickly the returner perceives the flight path of the ball and where she contacts the ball in relation to her body (i.e., is it comfortably in front or too close to her body?). Her contact point will often give a big clue as to how well she reads the game generally. If she continually hits the ball too close to her, then she probably doesn't perceive the oncoming ball in enough time, causing her to prepare too late for the shot. More work will be needed on her receiving skills if this is the case.

DRILL 2.2 **Neutralising With the Inside-Out Return**

AIM
To neutralise the threat of the first serve by developing inside-out returns from the forehand and backhand sides.

LEVEL
All

DESCRIPTION
Returning targets (measuring 1.8 × 1.8 meters [6 × 6 feet]) are placed on the court for the player to aim for using the inside-out return from both sides. The coach (or practice partner) hits a number of first serves down the middle of the court for the player to practice against. Again, the player(s) should keep a score regarding the number of returns that neutralise the server's advantage.

VARIATION
As they develop this shot, players play practice points using only first serves hit down the middle from both the deuce and advantage courts. The returner is allowed to play the point out only if she manages to neutralise the serve completely using the inside-out return—that is, if she has at least a 50:50 chance of winning the point after the serve and return have been played. She is awarded three points if she manages to turn defence into attack by winning the point within her next two shots. The server should hit the occasional wide serve to prevent the returner from anticipating the middle serve too early.

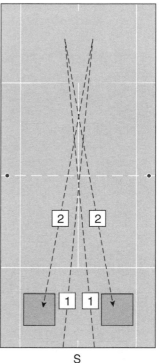

Inside-out returning targets hit against the middle serve from the deuce and advantage courts.

COACHING POINTS
The server should catch the ball immediately if she thinks the return is not effective enough. This is an excellent drill to test her perception skills because she must recognise the characteristics of the return quickly (i.e., its direction, height, depth, spin, and speed) and make a decision instantly. Coaches can increase the ratio (e.g., from 50:50 to 70:30) if the returner is dominating too often, or decrease the ratio if the server still holds too much advantage. This tool allows the coach to balance differences in playing standards between players while still maintaining a challenging environment for everyone. (These ratios are only approximate and subjective, of course, but they can be the source of lively debate between players and coaches!)

DRILL 2.3   Using the Inside-In Return to Move the Server

This drill helps to further develop the across-the-body return and encourages the player to dominate the server by maintaining a strong, central court position.

AIMS
To move the server away from her central court position; to turn defence into attack immediately.

LEVEL
Intermediate to advanced

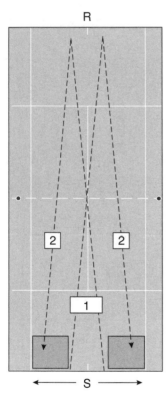

Inside-in returning targets hit against the middle serve from the deuce and advantage courts.

DESCRIPTION
The coach (or practice partner) hits a number of first serves down the middle of the court. The returner plays the point using the inside-in return from both her forehand and backhand sides. However, the point is played out only if the return forces the server to move two steps or more to the side. The drill is completed when the returner successfully moves the server five times from both returning sides.

VARIATION
Bonus points are awarded to the returner if she manages to win the point using a maximum of two more shots after the return. The server should be allowed to hit the wide serve occasionally to prevent the returner from anticipating the middle serve too early.

COACHING POINTS
The coach should encourage the returner to contact the oncoming ball in front of her body with a strong lower-body base. This strength prepares her for a strong 'collision' with the ball (i.e., a strong contact point) and will allow a more balanced recovery into the centre of the court. Developing such strong technique will give the returner the best chance to dominate her opponent from a first serve situation.

DRILL 2.4 Using the Blocked Return to Turn Defence Into Attack

AIMS
To neutralise the threat of a strong first serve; to turn defence into attack; to develop a feel for the ball.

LEVEL
All

DESCRIPTION
The coach (or practice partner) hits a mixture of first serves to a returner, who practices the blocked return using three specific targets to aim for. The main one is the deep, middle target, but there are also two short angle targets to aim for if she can control the threat of the wide serve well enough.

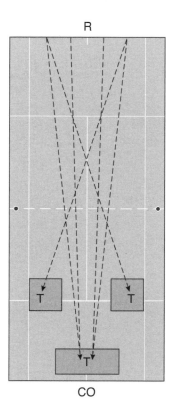

The deep, middle target and short angle targets used for the blocked return.

VARIATION
The player tries to hit two types of pace with her return: (1) the very slow paced block that forces the server to generate her own pace for her second shot and (2) the block that stays low and moves through the court at a faster pace, allowing the server less time to prepare for her next shot.

COACHING POINTS
Experimenting with different paces will help a player develop a feel for the ball. The coach should encourage the player to use the short angle block against the wide serve because there is more angle available compared to the middle serve. The coach should also note the position of the returner after the serve and return have been played. Has she neutralised well enough? Is she in a position to attack? Can she approach the net if her short angle block has forced her opponent out of court? This information can help the returner understand what her next move should be—that is, whether she should defend, build, or attack with her next shot.

DRILL 2.5   Returning From an Aggressive Court Position

AIMS
To practice hitting the ball at or just after the top of its bounce; to practice returning from an aggressive court position; to highlight where the second serve return could be played from; to improve perception of the oncoming serve.

LEVEL
All

DESCRIPTION
The returner places a marker where the second serve bounces in the service box and also where its *second* bounce lands. If the return is to be hit at the top of its bounce, then it follows that the returner should contact the ball exactly between these two markers. This middle distance is often well inside the baseline. The returner should try to contact the ball as close to the top of its bounce as possible and try to hit at least 7 out of 10 in this way. Each player should do this against 10 second serves and then rotate.

COACHING POINTS
Players often try to return aggressively, but from too far behind the baseline. The coach should encourage a more aggressive returning position, farther up the court, because with a weak second serve, its second bounce often lands inside the baseline as well! The coach should emphasise early preparation and simple technique, with a contact point in front of the body at all times to allow the player to transfer her body weight forward.

DRILL 2.6   Dominating With the Second Serve Return

This drill can be done with either singles or doubles.

AIMS
To practice the return and groundstroke attack; to make the returner select the best return and second shot option; to make the returner (or returning team) dominate the point.

LEVEL
All

DESCRIPTION
The returner (or returning team) has to win the point within three of her shots (including the return). If the returner hasn't won the point after three shots, the point stops immediately and the server wins the point. This forces the returner to seize the initiative of the rally straightaway. She will want to contact the return from inside the baseline and may choose to attack down the line to create an advantage.

VARIATIONS
1. If the returner hasn't won the point after three of her shots, the point is allowed to finish. If the returner wins the point after three shots, she does not score (i.e., she prevents the server from scoring). If the server wins a point at any time, she scores a point as normal.
2. The number of shots the returner is allowed can be increased or decreased depending on the level of play.
3. Coaches can combine this drill for both server and returner; that is, allow the server only three shots to win the point using her first serve and allow the returner only three shots using her second serve return.

COACHING POINTS
The returner should build the point with controlled aggression because three shots will often be enough to win the point with—especially against a weak second serve. When the point ends after the returner's third shot, the coach should note whether she is in a dominating, neutral, or defensive position. This will show how effective she is at using this tactic.

DRILL 2.7   Maintaining Baseline Control After the Return

AIMS
To maintain control over the opponent from the baseline through a series of pressuring groundstrokes hit after the second serve return; to enhance tactical awareness by noting the momentum of each rally.

LEVEL
All

DESCRIPTION
Players play first to seven points with the same player serving only second serves until completion. The returner must maintain dominance over her opponent by never giving her the chance to recover to a neutral position during the rally. This means that the returner must always be more than 50:50 ahead in the point. If the server manages to recover back to neutral, the returner loses the point automatically.

VARIATION
Players combine the first serve and control tactic with the second serve return and control tactic. In other words, when the first serve goes in, the server has to always remain in control of the point, but when she misses her first serve, the returner must maintain control instead.

COACHING POINTS
This drill will force the player to hit with more consistent aggression and will make her look for any opportunity to dominate her opponent. Players should be encouraged to play as many balls from inside the baseline as possible. The coach should note how quickly the player manages to perceive her own rally position—and how realistic her judgments are of neutral and dominating positions. Doing this will help to indicate how well she reads the game tactically and will encourage her to use more perception and anticipation skills in matches.

DRILL 2.8   Using the Drive Volley After the Return

AIMS
To practice the return and drive volley tactic; to make the returner dominate the point; to help the returner improve her anticipation and perception skills.

LEVEL
All

DESCRIPTION
The player uses a two-shot, crosscourt pattern to dominate her opponent. The coach hits second serves to the player, who returns aggressively crosscourt from either the deuce or advantage court. The coach defends this shot with a high, floated ball hit down the line (hand-fed if necessary). The player moves in and hits a drive volley crosscourt into the space. The drill is completed when the player hits five return and drive volley patterns from each returning side.

VARIATION
The coach feeds a variety of high second shots across the court so the returner has to decide quickly whether to drive volley with a forehand or backhand. The coach then feeds a variety of high and low balls, forcing the player to perceive the flight path of the ball quickly enough so that she can make the correct shot selection. Hitting a normal volley or short groundstroke against a low ball will be a better second shot choice.

COACHING POINTS
The returner must read the flight path of the ball quickly. She must decide whether to hit a forehand or backhand and move inside the baseline and position herself correctly. Again, a large target area should be encouraged for the drive volley. The coach should note where the player moves to after the drive volley. Does she naturally move in to the net, or does she prefer to move back to the baseline? Her movement will indicate where she is most comfortable playing from. If she prefers to come forward, then she could add a 'finish' volley to this aggressive pattern (i.e., a volley into the space that wins the point).

DRILL 2.9   Using the Sneak After the Return

AIMS
To practice the return and sneak tactic; to make the returner dominate the point; to develop efficient movement to the net; to help the returner improve her instinctive decision-making skills.

LEVEL
Intermediate to advanced

DESCRIPTION
The coach hits second serves to the player, who tries to return aggressively from inside the baseline. If the return puts the coach under pressure, then she must use the sneak and play her second shot as a volley. The player must play the volley from inside the service line each time. The drill should begin with the player knowing the direction of the serve beforehand and progress to a more open situation once the player has developed her execution of the tactic. The player completes the drill after five successful sneaks from each returning side.

VARIATION
Bonuses can be awarded when the player uses the return and sneak tactic. The coach rewards the player's correct instinct, even if she loses the point.

COACHING POINTS
The returner must be able to recognise two things quickly: (1) how her return is going to affect her opponent (anticipation) (i.e., as soon as the ball leaves her racket, she should have an idea as to how good the return is going to be) and (2) the type of shot her opponent has just played (perception) (i.e., is her second shot aggressive, defensive, or neutralising, and can it be volleyed?). The coach must match the second shot (which may be a hand-feed) with the quality of the return. For example, a powerful and early return, hit from well inside the baseline, should elicit a more defensive second shot. This gives the player realistic and natural feedback.

DRILL 2.10 Using the Return and Planned Approach

AIMS
To practice the return and planned approach tactic; to make the returner dominate the point; to develop efficient movement to the net; to help the returner increase her variety of shot.

LEVEL
Intermediate to advanced

DESCRIPTION
The coach hits second serves to the player's backhand side. The player must approach down the line, middle, or short crosscourt with either a topspin or slice return (use returning targets on court if possible). The coach plays his or her second shot down the middle of the court to give the player valuable volleying practice. The player must play this volley from inside the service line every time. The drill is completed when the player successfully uses both the chip and charge and drive-in approach five times each.

VARIATION
The point is played out normally once the return and planned approach tactic has been developed. The serve is hit to either the forehand or backhand side, and the coach's second shot can be played anywhere. Bonus points are awarded for successful execution of this tactic during practice matches. Also, the player should use the drop shot return to approach with to increase shot variety.

COACHING POINTS
The coach should note whether the player is more comfortable approaching with the forehand or backhand return, and if she prefers to hit with topspin or slice. The coach should also note which court she is more effective returning from (i.e., the deuce or advantage court), and whether she prefers the middle or wide serve to attack. Early perception of the oncoming serve will help the player prepare in time and contact the ball in front of her body. This, in turn, will allow her to move forward through the shot and approach more naturally in to the net. Once she establishes which planned approach she favours most, the coach should encourage her to incorporate it into her next match. This will help add tactical variety to her game.

DRILL 2.11 Developing the Return and Planned Approach in Doubles

AIMS
To practice the return and planned approach tactic; to make the returning team dominate the point; to develop coordinated movement at the net; to improve communication and teamwork between partners.

LEVEL
Intermediate to advanced

DESCRIPTION
The doubles team sets up in the normal one-up/one-back returning position while the coach stands on the opposite baseline in a serving position. The coach hits a second serve to the returner, who approaches behind her return. The coach hits or feeds a number of different second shots to the pair (e.g., down the middle, down the line, short crosscourt, lob, fast pace, slow pace). The aim of the drill is for the returning team to be able to recognise three things immediately: (1) Is the ball going in? (2) If so, whose shot is it? and (3) Where do they hit to? The returning team must hit to specific targets depending on the type of ball the coach hits to them. (For information on net play targets in doubles, see chapter 4.)

COACHING POINTS
The coach should encourage a safe target area positioned well inside the baseline for the returning team's second shot (probably a volley or smash unless a lob forces them back to the baseline). The coach must ensure that each player knows her area of the net to cover (e.g., who takes the lob down the middle?) and that both players move together, as one unit, at the net. The returner's partner at the net should start to move forward as her partner joins her, so both players are moving forward 'shoulder to shoulder'. This applies to sideways and backward movement also. This parallel play prevents any big gaps from opening up between them for the opposing team to hit into.

Playing the Baseline

The increased speed and strength of today's female players have allowed them to dominate with the serve and return. In addition, they are hitting groundstrokes harder, earlier, and with more purpose from the baseline than they did in previous years. As a result, the moments during a rally when both players play from a neutral position are becoming fewer and shorter. In fact, at any given moment during a baseline rally, each player will try to do one of only three things: build, attack, or defend against her opponent. Building can be defined as hitting one or more groundstrokes to create an opportunity to attack—which in turn means trying to create an opportunity to finish the point. Defending, on the other hand, involves trying to prevent the opponent from finishing the point. These three tactical objectives may well switch between players within the same point, and their baseline play will often become a tug-of-war—both players try to impose their own tactics on the other. This is when tennis is played at its entertaining best. This chapter studies the key factors involved in building, attacking, and defending from the baseline.

Building From the Baseline

Every successful tennis player uses a range of building shots from the baseline that help create a platform from which to attack. They are played when neither player holds an obvious advantage in the rally—usually when the threat of the serve or return has been nullified. Building shots simply make life difficult for an opponent. They are not meant to be hit as outright winners (like some attacking shots) but rather to force opponents to hit less comfortable shots from more awkward court positions. To do this, a player must learn how to build a rally from the baseline by using groundstrokes hit with consistency, accuracy, and variety.

Consistency

Top international-level players hit winning shots only 20 to 25 percent of the time. At lower levels of competition, this probably drops to about 10 to 15 percent. In other words, the majority of points in tennis are won through forced or unforced errors. This is a crucial point because many players believe they must constantly hit winning shots past their opponents and give little thought to how often the opponent actually misses! There can be no doubt that the game of tennis punishes inconsistency at every level, and this means that every player must *consistently* execute her shots and tactics well.

In 2006 Maria Sharapova won her first US Open title, beating Justine Henin-Hardenne in a thrilling final. The standard of tennis on show that day was extremely high, yet the number of winning shots played still remained relatively low. The percentage of winning shots hit overall was 22 (including serves that forced a return error), whereas the percentage of unforced errors was 35 (www.usopen.org). This ratio of winners to unforced errors is very common in tennis even at the highest level. Consistency, therefore, remains crucial to a player's ability to maintain control and build from the baseline in singles *and* doubles—whether following a serve, a return, or playing from a neutral rally position.

Playing consistently from the baseline doesn't mean playing defensively, however. Without a doubt, the defensive player who relies solely on an opponent's unforced errors will be severely restricted. Today's successful female players play aggressive, committed tennis without making a large number of unforced errors. In recent years, players such as Anastasia Myskina, Patty Schnyder, and Martina Hingis have all been known for making their opponents work exceptionally hard to beat them. Yet in no way do they play defensive tennis. In fact, most players now build opportunities to attack by using groundstrokes hit at a higher tempo than ever before. They hit harder and earlier and move faster to the ball without increasing their error count. Drill 3.3, later in this chapter, emphasises practicing at a high tempo while maintaining a sharp focus on consistency.

The following tips will help the coach emphasise consistency in each practice session:

• Play to a rally target. Starting the practice session with a 20-, 50-, or 100-shot rally can be rewarding for the player and coach—especially when the length of the rally increases over time. The idea is to set a challenging rally target without spending too much time trying to achieve it! Being able to rally without error enhances the player's confidence and improves concentration. This drill can inject strong positive energy into the start of any practice session.

• Count the warm-up errors. Counting her errors during her warm-up will automatically focus the player's mind at the beginning of her practice session. There is no need to place a consequence on the number of mistakes made. Simply being aware of these errors should prompt her to correct them naturally.

• Carry the net errors. In this drill, the player must carry all the balls she hits into the net on her person (e.g., in her pockets, down her socks). This fun exercise provides a physical reminder of how many net errors she has made. The coach must ensure that the player still hits with positive, committed technique instead of simply 'pushing' the ball over the net so as not to make a mistake.

- Allow only a certain number of errors. Being allowed only a certain number of errors, or 'lives', will help focus the player's mind and can conjure matchlike feelings of anxiety as she makes more errors. This drill can help the coach see how the player deals with tension and how well she is able to maintain consistency under pressure, which will be crucial for future match play. Much of modern tennis is about the relationship between errors and winners. In today's game it is totally acceptable for a player to make errors as long as the number of *quality* shots she hits far outweighs them. This idea should be reflected in the way this drill is set up. For example, by allowing five quality shots in court to cancel one unforced error, the player learns to respect this relationship and strives to achieve a positive ratio between quality shots and unforced errors.

- Winning with consistency. The player is awarded a point only when she wins two points in a row. Again, this drill rewards consistent performances in a competitive situation. This scoring system should be used for both players at the same time—whether serving or returning. Physical and mental stamina is required because each game can last for much longer than normal. (Players should keep alternating sides even if the score may not match the serving side. For example, the server will serve at 15–0 from the deuce court if she wins the first two points in a row.) The coach can alter the scoring system to balance differing playing standards and to put varying levels of pressure on each player if necessary. For example, the returner may be allowed to score normally while the server has to win two points in a row.

To improve consistency, see drills 3.1 through 3.3 on pages 107 through 109.

🎾 Coaching Tip

Many consistency drills involve counting the number of errors made. This can help a player concentrate because she knows she has only so many 'lives' left with which to play. However, this usually means that the last shot of the drill is an error; that is, the drill ends once the player has made a certain number of mistakes. Even if the player has played exceptionally well during the drill, it is natural for her to remember only the last shot—the shot that let her down. As Paul Dent, British national coach and sport psychologist, often says, 'Stop the drill after the good stuff!'

It is important, therefore, to sometimes provide a more positive experience for a player by setting consistency targets to achieve. For example, a block of 10 shots in a row can equal one point, and the drill can be changed when the player reaches a certain number of points. In this way the player finishes after a positive performance.

Accuracy

The importance of accuracy varies with different tactical requirements. Generally, the more qualities associated with a shot (e.g., pace, spin, variety), the less accurate the shot has to be because the opponent is under pressure in different ways. Therefore, building shots played from defensive and neutral positions must be more accurate than attacking shots played from offensive positions. This is because there is less chance that they can be played with other qualities such as pace, spin, variety, directional change, and early court position. This is particularly relevant to baseline play, in which a crosscourt, building groundstroke played from a neutral position needs to be more accurate than an aggressive, early, attacking one. Accuracy, therefore, remains a key ingredient to the baseline building shot.

An accurate building shot will often create an opportunity for a player to attack. One of the most popular ways for a player to make the transition from a neutral playing position on the baseline to an attacking one is to rally crosscourt until an opportunity to change direction by 'switching' down the line arises. Note that this switch shot down the line doesn't need to be hit with the same accuracy as the crosscourt shot because other factors put pressure on the opponent. The directional change, as well as the pace and early court position of the 'switcher', is often enough to pressure the opponent. In fact, it is common to see switch shots land on the service line and still force opponents into error. Figure 3.1 shows the accuracy required for the crosscourt building backhand compared to the switch down the line. Note how large the target area is for the switch shot because more qualities are attached to the shot—directional change, time pressure, added pace—compared to the crosscourt building backhand.

A common mistake made by less experienced players is to believe that the shot down the line must be hit for a winner. Even though they try to move from a

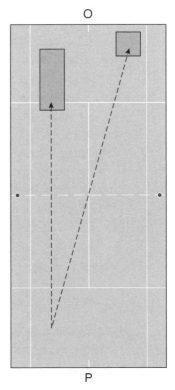

FIGURE 3.1 The target area required for the crosscourt building groundstroke compared to the switch shot, played down the line.

neutral position to an attacking one, players often lose the shape of their technique because they try to hit the ball too hard and close to the lines. When this happens, unforced errors occur when they shouldn't. Players must realise that the switch down the line is a wrong-footing shot that should be aimed well inside the court. The same principle applies when switching down the line from either the backhand or forehand side.

Coaching Tip

The coach should encourage a player to maintain a 20 percent variation of shot direction. In other words, changing the direction of the ball one in five times is enough to create tactical uncertainty for an opponent.

Choosing when to transition from neutral to attack is crucial and will always depend on the quality of the building shot played before it. This principle applies to all baseline tactics. For example, when using the switch tactic, the more accurate the crosscourt backhand is, the better the chance of receiving a shorter, slower ball that can be hit down the line. Having enough time to execute this shot is important along with the court position of the switcher because changing the direction of the ball from too deep a position will increase the chance of error. Statistics produced by Craig Tiley and presented at the LTA Grand Slam Seminar 2004 show that there is actually an 80 percent increase in the chance of error when hitting down the line from a deep position, whereas there is no increase in the chance of error when hitting back crosscourt. Therefore, knowing when to switch (i.e., when a player is balanced and holding a strong court position) and understanding that this shot needs to be hit into a larger target area to allow for this increased risk remains crucial.

Drills 3.4 through 3.7 on pages 110 through 115 emphasise the accuracy and consistency required for building effectively from the baseline. All of them can be used with one, two, or three players on court and a variety of scoring systems to suit the level of each player.

Variety

I felt tactically, I played very well today, and also throughout the tournament, because my game is really different from what the other girls are playing on grass.

—Amelie Mauresmo after winning Wimbledon in 2006

There is certainly less variety used in the women's game today than in the past, because players hit the ball harder, flatter, and from a more aggressive court position without using a great amount of spin. Whether playing with variety is a thing of the past or future is an interesting debate. Nevertheless, a player who can effectively offer something *different* can gain an advantage. A building shot that is hit with a different type of spin or into an unfamiliar area of the court can be extremely effective. A player who has used such variety to create numerous attacking opportunities in recent years has been Justine Henin-Hardenne. Being able to hit with such great slice and topspin from the backhand side has allowed her to pressure her opponents through accuracy, consistency, and variety. Justine's technique allows her to play a number of different shots from the baseline, such as the aggressive backhand drive, the slice or topspin short angle, the slice or topspin recovery shot, and the drop shot. All of these building shots allow her to make the transition from neutral to attack.

The ability to hit with slice and topspin allows a player to play with more creativity from the baseline because she has more shot options available to her. However, not many players can hit both particularly well—especially those who hit with a double-handed backhand (who represent the majority of players on the WTA Tour). Girls who grow up hitting with two hands often do not have the strength to develop the single-handed slice (and backhand volley) until later in their careers and usually lack confidence hitting these shots as a result.

It is important to remember also that girls don't always have the same amount of time to develop their shots as boys do, which further hinders their creativity. The fact that girls mature faster than boys allows them to compete with older players much earlier because their physical differences are not as great. Therefore, they have a smaller window of opportunity to develop their game before senior competition becomes a reality. Perhaps this is one of the reasons we don't see a variety of building shots being hit from the baseline. Despite the great need for variety, most top women choose to play a few shots really well rather than a lot of shots fairly well.

Coaches should not underestimate the challenges that must be met to add variety to a young girl's game. However, there is no question that the ability to create different shots throughout a match can be a powerful weapon, because they can often disrupt an opponent's rhythm and concentration. They also allow the player to build a rally in a variety of ways, allowing the use of different tactics depending on the game style of her opponent. Shots such as the short angle, aggressive loop, absorbing slice, and drop shot will do exactly this and should be introduced and developed at an early age if they are to be used with confidence later on.

Short Angle   The ability to drag an opponent off the court through the use of the short angle is one of the main advantages held by a player who plays with variety. This shot is hit to a shorter and wider target on the court than the regular groundstroke is, luring the opponent away from the centre of the court into a less familiar position. When played effectively, this shot allows a player to finish the point in a number of ways, including using the sneak volley, drive volley, and shoulder-high groundstroke attack. The short angle can be played with either slice or topspin.

The short angle slice can be used to great effect if the ball stays short and low enough. This shot can cause an opponent two particular problems. First, it forces her to move diagonally up the court—a line of movement that is rarely practiced and often proves problematic. Second, the slice keeps the ball low and forces the opponent to hit 'up' over the net, thus preventing any real threat of aggression. Players will often approach or sneak in to the net after building pressure through the use of this shot.

The short angle topspin can be hit from the forehand and backhand side. It requires a player to hit the ball with fast racket head speed and a sharper brushing action up the back of the ball to create the necessary spin and angle. This shot presents a different problem to an opponent in that the topspin 'kicks' the ball out and away from the court, pulling the opponent out of the court and thus leaving the rest of the court exposed (see figure 3.2). When hit effectively, the short angle topspin groundstroke also creates many attacking opportunities for a player. It is important to note that it is harder for a player to create a short angle from the middle of the court because fewer angles are available. Therefore, most angled groundstrokes are hit from wider positions.

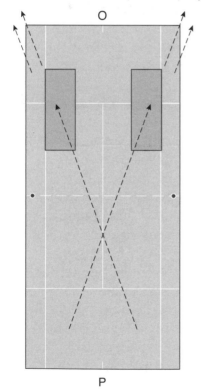

FIGURE 3.2 Target areas for the short angle groundstroke.

Drills 3.8 and 3.9 on pages 116 and 117 encourage players to use the short angle groundstroke, among a variety of other shots, because of the limited target areas on the court. In drill 3.8, the short angle must be hit more often because hitting into the middle of the court is forbidden. In drill 3.9, being restricted from hitting into one of the squares (particularly one of the two deep squares) will again encourage the use of the short angle groundstroke.

Aggressive Loop The aggressive loop is used to change the pace of a rally and to potentially break an opponent's rhythm. It should be hit aggressively with fast racket head speed, brushing up the back of the ball, just like a topspin lob (unlike a defensive 'moon ball' that floats over the net). The aggressive loop is most effective when played high and deep into the opponent's corner, especially to the backhand side of a single-handed player. It is often played as a way of approaching or sneaking in to the net because it pushes the opponent deep behind the baseline, allowing the player to move from a neutral to an attacking position. It is used most effectively on slow, hard or clay courts, because the higher-bouncing ball will push the opponent farther back and out of the court.

The aggressive loop is most effective when hit crosscourt because the player has more space to hit the ball into (i.e., the crosscourt direction is longer than down the line). The crosscourt angle also helps to pull the opponent deep and wide of the court. This shot is very difficult to dominate against and often results in a defensive return that can be attacked. The shoulder-high groundstroke attack, sneak, and drive volley are tactical options to be used if the aggressive loop has been played well enough. It also allows a player to develop more feel from the baseline because the aggressive loop teaches a different type of pace, spin, and height than does a conventional groundstroke. Tactical awareness is enhanced because this shot provides an alternative option against an opponent who keeps a consistently good length from the baseline.

To practice the aggressive loop, see drill 3.10 on page 118.

Absorbing Slice   The absorbing slice is a shot played mostly during the 'neutral' moments in a rally. It is used to absorb the pace of an opponent's groundstroke and keep the player firmly in the point until an attacking opportunity arises. The key to this shot lies in a player's ability to 'soak up' the pace of her opponent's shot with good timing and feel. Usually played from the backhand side (although some women are also beginning to use the forehand slice when forced out wide), the absorbing slice is hit between knee and waist height with a simple, efficient swing. Shot selection is crucial because it is difficult to play this shot from too high above the waist, particularly for players who normally hit with two hands on the backhand side. It is most effective when played deep and down the middle of the court because it offers an opponent neither pace nor angle. Opponents who try to create something with this ball can often make errors because they have little pace to work with, and the slice that stays low and deep enough can force them to hit short, thus creating an opportunity to attack.

To practice the tactics described in this section, see drill 3.11 on page 119.

Drop Shot   The drop shot is a highly underrated weapon that is delightful to watch when played well. It is most effective when played with disguise, and it is used when the opponent least expects it. Surprise is a winning tactic. Drop shots can be played from either side, and players often prefer their forehand groundstroke moving around their backhand to hit inside-out and inside-in drop shots. A player will disguise this shot by shaping up to hit a dominant forehand by using the same backswing but will alter the angle of her racket face and come under the ball at the last moment of her forward swing. Players who hit the backhand slice will enjoy hitting the drop shot from this side also because the technique used, and the feel required, are very similar. Again, a player will try to keep her backswing the same yet subtly abbreviate her forward swing so that the ball drops short.

Playing the drop shot down the line or middle will reduce the angles available to the opponent. Doing so also allows for greater accuracy because there is less distance for the ball to travel. This is an important point because players will always be able to hit a more accurate shot the closer they are to their intended target. This target, however, does not always have to be close to the line or net because it is often the surprise element that wrong-foots an opponent.

Finally, being able to show an opponent the ability to play the drop shot is important because, whether successful or not, it will help to disrupt an opponent's rhythm and increase uncertainty. One or two well-timed drop shots can often be enough to slow an opponent's response time because she has to prepare for more than one shot option. As a result, the rest of a player's baseline game will become more effective.

To practice disguising the drop shot, see drill 3.12 on page 119.

🎾 Coaching Tip

The coach can have players play points without a ball. Both players shadow a baseline rally, trying to incorporate as many different building shots into the rally as possible. Each player must anticipate the direction of her opponent's shadow shot to score a point. Players can progress to anticipating direction, depth, and spin as they become more accomplished. Again, the coach should encourage variety and disguise as much as possible.

To play with variety, a player must develop a feel for the ball and good control of the racket head. She will constantly change her swing, her contact point, and the angle of her racket face to play a range of shots. Visualising these shots by shadow-swinging without the ball can be an effective practice because it allows the player to focus solely on the *feel* of each shot. She should be encouraged to shadow-swing on the court, in front of a mirror, and with her eyes shut to increase her awareness of how every shot feels.

'Touch and feel' is about knowing how much force to apply. Tennis, first and foremost, is a control game. The concepts of feel and touch underlie control. The ability to make fine changes in the racket trajectory, its angle, and the amount and direction of its force is common in all so-called talented players. Players who execute specialty shots with consistent success have a fine sensitivity regarding the application of force and its timing. They appear to have an uncanny understanding and appreciation of gravity, which allows them to play lobs and floated backhand slice shots that consistently land close to the baseline (Dent and Hagelauer 2001).

Attacking From the Baseline

The boundaries between building and attacking shots can often merge, especially in the women's game. In other words, exactly when a player stops building and starts attacking during a rally is not always clear, particularly when a player continually hits aggressively from the baseline on a fast surface. A building shot is generally defined as a shot (or series of shots) that creates an opportunity to attack (i.e., a shot that creates a short ball, a slower ball, or a space). An attacking shot is then used to exploit this advantage. Many building shots, however, are good enough to force an opponent into error on their own merit, and this makes the two tactical intentions harder to distinguish between in some cases.

Remember that attacking from the baseline should not be defined as hitting outright winners. Instead, today's attacking baseline player aims to make her opponent *defend* in a way that forces her into error. Winners are by-products of the pressure applied. After all, statistics show that up to 85 percent of points are won through forced and unforced errors alone—a crucial point that coaches must emphasise whenever possible. Spaces open up on the court as an opponent is put under increasing pressure until something naturally gives way; either a winner or (more likely) an error finishes the point.

Today's top female players maintain a very high quality of shot from the beginning of a rally. Starting with a serve or a return, and continuing with a mix of building and attacking shots, they simply maintain their standard until their aggressive play is rewarded—as opposed to continually trying to hit better shots as the rally progresses. A good player will maintain the quality of her shot as she attacks her opponent from the baseline, no matter how long the rally lasts. A less experienced player will often try to play 'too well' the longer the rally continues—usually making an error as a consequence.

To attack successfully from the baseline, a player must be prepared to play from an aggressive court position and often hit the ball at shoulder height to maximise her dominance. She must also be ready to use the counterpunch as an attacking tactic at various times. These three factors are now considered in more detail.

Court Position

Many claim that a player's WTA ranking can be accurately predicted by watching her court position alone. Generally, players ranked in the top 100 play most of their groundstrokes from on or inside the baseline. Players ranked between 100 and 200 play from on or just outside the baseline, and players ranked below 200 play from farther back. Despite its simplicity, this view provides an interesting frame of reference because it is much harder to dominate an opponent from a position deep behind the baseline. This is not necessarily the case on the ATP Tour, however, because men have the strength to create a more 'viscous' spin on the ball that pulls an opponent off the court more effectively. They can do this from deeper and wider positions than their female counterparts can. Women generally hit the ball flatter than men do and, therefore, become less effective when playing from too deep. Their flatter groundstrokes cannot create as much angle or variety and will trouble their opponent less because of this. They are far more dangerous when playing from farther up the court, where an aggressive groundstroke, played on the rise or at the top of the bounce, will be rewarded more often. Hitting the ball at this trajectory will ensure efficient movement to every shot as well as an aggressive court position—the player hits many balls from inside the baseline. Following are some advantages to playing the game from inside the baseline:

© Sport The Library

Playing groundstrokes from inside the baseline will increase the pressure on an opponent.

- Hitting the ball earlier will give an opponent less time to prepare for her next shot.
- A player can use the pace from her opponent's previous shot more significantly, because the ball travels faster.
- Because she can use her opponent's pace, a player doesn't have to generate as much pace herself. She becomes more energy efficient.
- A player can be more accurate because she is closer to her chosen target.
- Different angles are available.
- Playing from inside the baseline allows a player easier access to the net (because there is less ground to cover).
- A strong, psychological message is often sent when playing from inside the baseline. Such aggressive tactical intent may force an opponent to make unwanted changes to her game.

A doubles pair that has exceptional groundstrokes can use the tactic of playing from on or inside the baseline also. Often used when returning, both players stay at the back and hit aggressive groundstrokes that apply consistent pressure to the serving team through pace, accuracy, and a lack of time. Because there is less space to hit into (two players on the opposite court instead of one), the baseline players simply use their opponents as targets. Both players look to move up the court together whenever a short ball or volley presents itself.

Both singles and doubles players who play well from on or inside the baseline have the following factors in common: They have excellent perception skills (i.e., they perceive the ball quickly and move immediately); their groundstrokes are hit with simple and efficient technique; they move quickly and are well balanced; and they bring a first-strike, proactive mentality to the court.

To practice the tactics discussed in this section, see drills 3.13 through 3.16 on pages 120 through 122.

Shoulder-High Attack

A player must be able to hit the ball at shoulder height if she is to attack effectively from the baseline. Hitting the ball early and aggressively from this position will simply increase the time and pace pressure applied to an opponent, forcing her to defend from a deeper position and increasing the chance of her making an error. Knowing that any shot that bounces short and high may be punished will force an opponent to hit closer to the lines, increasing the chance of error once more.

The shoulder-high attack allows a player to finish the point without letting her opponent back into the rally. It can be hit from the forehand or backhand side and requires a player to move very close to the oncoming bounce. It should be hit at shoulder height so that she still has the pace of the ball to work with. If the ball is allowed to bounce too high (i.e., above the player's head), then all pace and control may be lost.

This shot is often referred to as being part of a player's 'end game'. It is the shot that repeatedly finishes off a well-constructed point. The attacking baseline player must possess this if she is to profit from the opportunities that she creates from the baseline.

To practice the shoulder-high attack, see drill 3.17 on page 123.

Counterpunching

The counterpunch tactic is becoming increasingly common in the women's game as players are learning how to use the power their opponent gives them. This tactic is vital for the player who finds it hard to generate pace herself, because it allows her to attack with the pace of the oncoming ball instead. In this tactic, the pace of the ball is absorbed and directed back toward the opponent through good timing, simple technique, and excellent movement. The counterpunch tactic also requires an aggressive mentality, played with a measure of patience, because the player must wait for the right ball to attack with.

Players using the counterpunch tactic must perceive, react, and move to the ball very quickly. They should enjoy hitting aggressively on the run because the power player will want to dominate them as much as possible. Often, the counterpuncher will favour hitting on the run from a certain side and will deliberately leave this side open to tempt her opponent to hit there. Counterpunchers usually like a target to aim for also and will lure an opponent in to the net to pass or lob them. This is done by using drop shots and short angles and leaving the 'obvious' space open for the opponent to attack and approach into.

The tactic of deliberately bringing an opponent in to the net is often used in doubles also. This tactic can be very successful, particularly when used against a weak volleyer, because it presents the baseline player with an obvious target to aim for. As long as the deliberate short ball stays low, this will force the opposing player (or pair) to approach the net and hit high over it, setting up the aggressive passing shot or lob.

Remember that the counterpunch tactic is an attacking one and can be used by the power player also, even if not all her shots are hit with pace from the baseline. In fact, some players will deliberately take pace off the ball to slow the tempo of a rally down before stepping up and hitting with power when an opponent least expects it.

Elena Dementieva demonstrated classic counterpunching ability throughout 2004 when she was having major serving problems. On some occasions her serve speed was recorded as low as 91 km/h (57 mph). However, knowing that her opponent was certain to attack her serve, Elena geared herself up to counterattack with a high-quality, aggressive, and accurate second shot that often caught her opponent off guard. Elena reached two Grand Slam finals in 2004.

In recent years, players such as Martina Hingis, Anastasia Myskina, and Patty Schnyder have regularly used the counterpunching tactic to great effect. Without a doubt, the modern-day counterpuncher who is fast, aggressive, and technically versatile is evolving as a foil to the power player. When the two meet, it can make for the most entertaining match-up in tennis!

To practice the counterpunch tactic, see drill 3.18 on page 124.

Defending From the Baseline

She was defending all the balls pretty deep, and even with her slice, it kept coming really low. It was hard for me to get under those and try to go for winners from there.

—Kim Clijsters after losing to Justine Henin-Hardenne in the French Open Semi-Finals in 2006

The ability to defend from the baseline has become crucial in women's tennis because players are increasingly looking to build and attack from the start of the point. As a result, defending effectively means neutralising an opponent's threat immediately.

The ability to defend should not be confused with that of playing a defensive game style (which is rarely seen nowadays). Even the most dominant player will find herself defending at certain moments during a match, yet it is this part of the game that is often neglected in favour of creating power. Coaches must remember that tennis is as much about *receiving* power as it is about sending it.

Following are some points to consider when developing defensive skills:

- Players must know their own limitations. An attackable ball for one may be a defendable ball for another.

- A player's need to defend doesn't have to last long. This may mean playing only a handful of defensive shots in a game, set, or match.
- Effective shot-making can turn a defensive position into an attacking one immediately.
- Players hitting more than two defensive shots in a row usually lose the point.
- Perception and decision making are just as important as technique and movement. The earlier the player can perceive the oncoming ball, the quicker her decision will be, and the more competent her execution will be. Many players do not recognise the need to defend until it is too late.
- Players must accept the need to defend at times. Some players find it hard to accept that they have to hit more mundane-looking shots to stay in the point. It seems that they would rather 'miss looking mighty' than 'defend looking dull'!

A player will be required to defend from a number of different court positions. Her position will directly influence the type of defensive shot that she chooses to hit. Her choice of shot will also depend greatly on the positioning and tactical intention of her opponent. The following defensive shots will offer her a range of choices, allowing her the best possible chance of neutralising the playing situation she is in.

Recovery Shot

The recovery shot is hit when a player has been forced out of position from the baseline (either deep or wide, or both). The type of recovery shot that she hits will depend upon how much pressure she is under and what she expects her opponent to do next. Her two main recovery shot options are to hit the ball high and deep or deliberately low over the net.

Being able to hit the high recovery shot is vital for a player who is being attacked from the baseline. It is used to neutralise an opponent's advantage and differs from the low recovery shot because it is played with much height and spin over the net. It is usually played either deep down the middle of the court to reduce the angles available to an opponent or deep crosscourt to allow a very high margin of error (see figure 3.3 for the target area). When played well, the height, spin, and depth of the shot bring valuable recovery time to a player who finds herself under pressure. The high recovery shot is intended to neutralise an opponent's advantage immediately; if it is hit well enough, a defensive position could become an attacking one straightaway. A player can create a psychological advantage if she hits the recovery shot consistently well, because her opponent can become increasingly frustrated at failing to take advantage of her dominant position. The opponent's expectation of success increases as she senses the 'finish line' at the end of the point, yet an effective recovery shot will keep her from crossing it. This can result in an opponent forcing her shots even more, leading to her making more errors than normal as she experiences thoughts of 'I should have . . .', 'I could have . . .', and 'If only . . .'.

The low recovery shot is a defensive shot that is hit low over the net when a player is out of position. This shot has recently evolved as an alternative defensive option. It is played against the attacking baseline player who is comfortable attacking the high recovery shot with a drive volley, sneak volley, or smash. The low recovery shot carries a higher risk because it is hit low over the net and, more often, down the line, making it harder to attack and approach against. The low, short, crosscourt recovery shot is another effective version that can be used against the attacking player who doesn't move up the court very well. This player may deal with the high recovery shot easily because she is comfortable playing from shoulder height, yet she may struggle to attack the lower, shorter ball. Note the direction of the down-the-line shot. The ball travels toward the *inside* of the court rather than the outside of the court. This maintains a higher margin of error because the player aims to hit around the outside edge of the ball, bringing it back into play. Figure 3.4 shows the target areas for the low recovery shot. This shot is best played either deep down the line or short crosscourt. The low recovery shot can be hit with either topspin or slice, although the slice is preferred by many because its bounce stays lower, becoming harder to attack as a result. Kim Clijsters made this shot famous by regularly defending from a wide position with her forehand slice—while doing the splits!

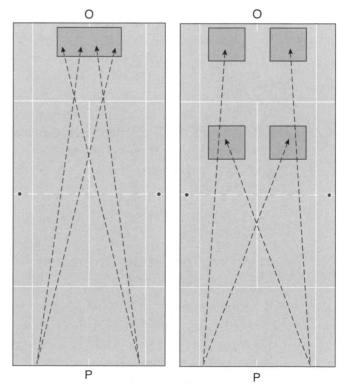

FIGURE 3.3 Target areas for the high recovery shot.

FIGURE 3.4 Target areas for the low recovery shot.

To practice the tactics discussed in this section, see drills 3.19 through 3.21 on pages 125 through 127.

Coaching Tip

The coach can assign different tactical roles during points play. Players can try to build, attack, or defend for certain periods. Coaches can also assign younger players a top player to try to copy (e.g., 'Can you play like Venus?'). Their opponents then try to guess who they are trying to play like. It is very interesting to note the role that suits each player best.

In doubles, a returning pair may also choose to defend from the baseline when they are consistently put under pressure from a strong serving pair that enjoys attacking from the net. The tactic of both players staying back when facing a first serve point is quite common. The returner's partner usually moves forward to a net position for a second serve point because less pressure is expected. This 'both back' formation completely changes the look of the court and can often force the serving pair into making more errors. The key point here is that the serving pair no longer has any specific volley targets to aim for when facing both players on the baseline, whereas the one-up/one-back formation allows the pair to volley behind or straight at the opposing net player. By standing on the baseline, both players are in a good position to defend any type of volley or smash, as long as they can move up the court quickly enough to defend against the short angle and drop volley. This formation, therefore, is particularly effective on slower courts where a player has more time to reach each ball. Knowing all this may force the attacking pair to play even more aggressively, increasing the chance of error.

To practice defending as a team, see drill 3.22 on page 128.

Defending Against the Drop Shot

A number of options are available for a player to defend against an opponent's drop shot, depending on how much pressure she is under. Obviously a player's first priority is to reach the drop shot and make her opponent play another shot. This may be her only goal if she is under intense pressure. However, sometimes a player is put under less pressure and can choose which type of shot to play. Following are examples of such situations.

If the opponent has hit the drop shot but remained on the baseline, a player generally has two options. First, if she can reach the ball in time, she can play the ball down the line and maintain a strong net position. This would force her opponent to create an angle in order to pass or lob her. The down-the-line option is preferable to the crosscourt option from this position because the crosscourt reply gives an opponent the chance to hit a passing shot into the natural space down the line. Figure 3.5 shows the options available to an opponent when a player has defended either down the line or crosscourt against the drop shot. When the player hits down the line, the opponent has to create a space to hit into. However, when the player hits crosscourt, the opponent already has a natural space to hit into. The player's second option is to drop shot back if she sees her opponent staying on the baseline. This tactic becomes more effective the deeper an opponent's court position is. Again, it is preferable to play the drop shot back down the line, rather than crosscourt, because of the reduced angle available.

If an opponent hits the drop shot and follows it in to the net, the player has three options. She can try to hit the ball past her opponent on either side; she can try to play the lob; or she can try to hit the ball straight at her opponent. The execution of these shots obviously depends on the quality of the drop shot and the pressure the player is under. Hitting to either side of an opponent can be effective as long as the shot stays low and away from the natural swing path of an opponent's volley. It is preferable to play the lob only if it can be hit aggressively; otherwise, a player will quickly become a sitting duck. Playing straight at an opponent will offer her fewer angles and can catch her by surprise.

To practice defending against the drop shot, see drill 3.23 on page 129.

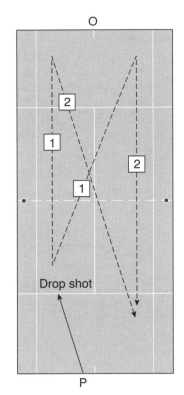

FIGURE 3.5 Defending down the line versus crosscourt against the drop shot, when an opponent remains on the baseline.

Assessing Baseline Play

There are a number of ways to measure how effective a player is from the baseline. The results of these methods provide important objective feedback to a player, help to highlight her strengths and limitations, and are vital to refer to when evaluating and setting goals for the season. The following three methods are most commonly used: a match flow chart, a court diagram, and baseline percentages.

Using a match flow chart is one of the most popular methods of recording information from matches. A graph is used (preferably drawn on graph paper). Starting from the centre, an X (or dot) is marked *up* for every point won, and an X is marked *down* for every point lost. The Xs are connected with a line to show the 'flow' (or momentum) of the match. Figure 3.6 shows the type of information that can be recorded on a flow chart. Note how the Xs have been replaced by numbers, which represent the rally length for each point. In this sample chart, the top line (S or R) denotes serve and return games; the second line (e.g., 2–1) denotes the match score; the third line (1, 2, or 0) denotes a first serve point, second serve point, or double fault; the fourth line (!) denotes game points; and the fifth line (√) denotes any specific positive performance, while (?) denotes missed opportunities or areas for improvement. The numbers on the graph denote the length of rally (0 being a double fault), and the lines that join each number denote the flow of the match (i.e., line up = point won; line down = point lost).

A match flow chart can be used to highlight any of the four performance factors in tennis (i.e., tactics, technique, physical conditioning, and mental skills). From a tactical perspective, specific baseline patterns of play can be charted using symbols (e.g., √!?). For example, √ may

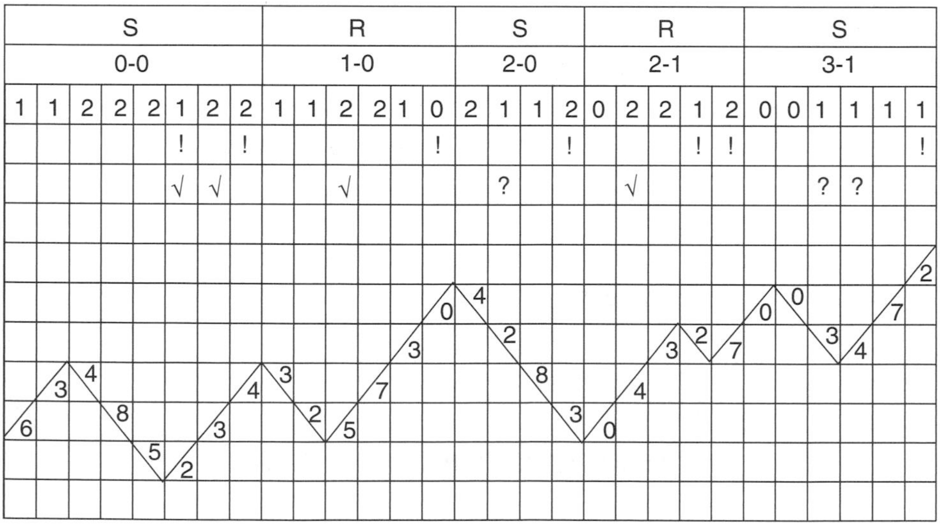

S								R						S				R					S					
0-0								1-0						2-0				2-1					3-1					
1	1	2	2	2	1	2	2	1	1	2	2	1	0	2	1	1	2	0	2	2	1	2	0	0	1	1	1	1
				!		!							!				!				!	!						!
			√	√						√						?				√						?	?	

FIGURE 3.6 Example of a match flow chart.

mean that variety of shot was used to good effect or that the shoulder-high attack was executed well. In addition, statistics such as the average length of rally and serve or return effectiveness can also be recorded. Specific notes should also be written underneath the chart to highlight key tactical moments during the match. These notes will help to back up any statistical information that has been gathered.

A court diagram is often used as an effective visual tool to highlight tactical factors such as consistency, accuracy, and variety. The coach simply marks an X on the court diagram where a player's shot lands. This could be used to highlight the accuracy of one specific shot (e.g., an inside-out forehand) or a more general group of shots (e.g., the depth of all groundstrokes), providing very specific feedback that can be used to set future performance goals. It could even be used to chart an opponent's shots (e.g., the direction of all first serves), the results of which could be used for future reference. A player's court position could also be highlighted by marking an X where she hits the ball from, rather than where she hits the ball to. Figure 3.7 shows a court diagram that charts the accuracy and consistency of a right-handed player's backhand crosscourt building groundstroke. A total of 22 backhands have been charted, and the player has hit 13 into court. She has made three net errors, two wide errors, and four deep errors. This pattern shows that the player often hits her backhand to a good length (11 shots hit past the service line), yet she needs to improve the width of this shot to create more attacking opportunities by moving her opponent away from the centre of the court.

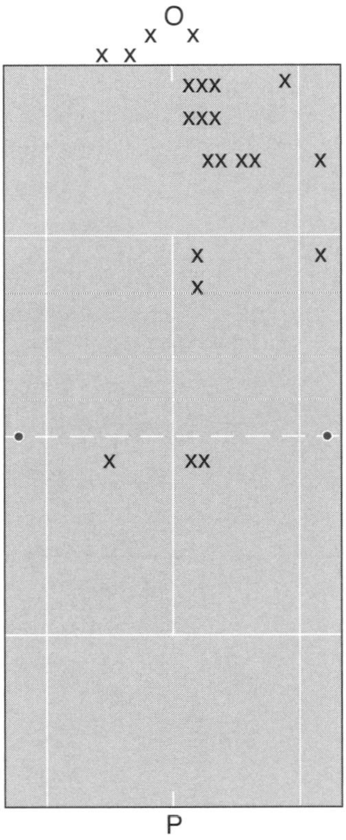

FIGURE 3.7 An example of a court diagram.

Finally, information regarding the effectiveness of a player's baseline play can be recorded in percentages, the same way serve, return, and net play statistics are. This information will allow the player and coach to analyse the effectiveness of the player's baseline play in a very objective way. Figure 3.8 is a baseline summary. To calculate the various percentage statistics that help indicate a player's baseline performance, divide the first number in the sequence by the second number and multiply by 100.

Baseline Summary

_____ (number of forehands or backhands hit in) / _____ (number of forehand or backhand attempts)

= _____ percentage of forehands or backhands in

_____ (number of baseline points won using shoulder-high attack) / _____ (total number of shoulder-high attack points played)

= _____ percentage of shoulder-high attack attempts that were successful

_____ (number of groundstrokes hit from inside the baseline) / _____ (total number of groundstrokes hit)

= _____ percentage of groundstrokes hit from inside the baseline

_____ (number of points won using variety from the baseline) / _____ (total number of baseline variety points played)

= _____ percentage of attempts at using variety from the baseline that were successful

_____ (number of neutralising defensive shots) / _____ (total number of defensive shots played)

= _____ percentage of defensive shots that neutralised immediately

_____ (number of successful building or attacking shots hit) / _____ (total number of groundstrokes hit)

= _____ percentage of groundstrokes that forced the opponent to defend

FIGURE 3.8 Baseline summary.

Summary

☐ At any given moment during a baseline rally, each player will do one of three things: build, attack, or defend against her opponent. Building can be defined as hitting one or more groundstrokes to create an opportunity to attack, which in turn means trying to create an opportunity to finish the point. Defending involves trying to prevent the opponent from finishing the point.

☐ Most points are won through forced or unforced errors. Consistency, therefore, is a crucial factor and should remain at the core of every player's ability to maintain control and build from the baseline in singles and doubles.

☐ The importance of accuracy varies with different tactical requirements. Generally, the more qualities that are associated with a shot (e.g., pace, spin, variety, etc.), the less accurate the shot has to be because the opponent is put under pressure in different ways.

☐ Today's female tennis players use less variety than past players. Players are hitting the ball harder, flatter, and from a more aggressive court position, without using a great amount of spin. However, those players who offer something different can gain an advantage because they can use shots that throw off an opponent's rhythm. These shots include the short angle (hit with slice or topspin), the aggressive loop, the absorbing slice, and the drop shot.

☐ To attack successfully from the baseline, a player must make her opponent defend in such a way that she is forced into error. Experienced players simply maintain a high quality of shot throughout a rally rather than continually try to hit better shots as time goes on. This applies equally to singles and doubles play.

☐ Women tend to attack from farther inside the baseline than men do (who can use more spin from farther behind the baseline). There are a number of advantages to playing from this position.

☐ To play from inside the baseline, a player needs to possess excellent perception skills, simple and efficient stroke technique, fast and balanced movement, and a first-strike mentality. She should also be able to comfortably attack the ball at shoulder height to maintain the time and pace pressure applied to her opponent.

☐ Some players learn how to counterpunch against the power player by using the pace of the oncoming ball to attack with. Power players also use this tactic by deliberately taking pace off the ball, only to surprise their opponent with added pace later in the rally.

☐ Defending from the baseline requires a player to neutralise an opponent's threat immediately. This can be done using the high recovery shot (in which the height, spin, and depth of the ball allow a player valuable time to recover back into the court) and the low recovery shot (which is used to counter an opponent who approaches the net more often or an opponent who doesn't like playing against a low bouncing ball).

☐ In doubles, a pair may choose to defend by having both players play from the baseline. This can often change the look of the court and can force the opposing pair at the net to try too hard on their volleys and smashes.

☐ When a player defends against the drop shot, her first priority is to reach it and make her opponent play another shot. If she can do this comfortably, then her options depend on where her opponent is positioned. If her opponent is on the baseline, she can either play down the line (forcing her opponent to create an angle past her) or drop shot back. If her opponent follows the drop shot in to the net, she could try to hit past her, lob her, or play straight at her.

☐ There are a number of ways to measure how effective a player is from the baseline. The results of these methods will help to high-light a player's strengths and limitations and will be vital to refer to when evaluating and setting goals for the season. The three most common methods used are a match flow chart, a court diagram, or playing statistics that convert into percentages.

DRILL 3.1 Counting the Quality Shots

AIMS
To practice hitting a number of quality shots in a row; to develop a personal definition of a quality shot.

LEVEL
All

DESCRIPTION
The player is asked to hit a certain number of quality shots within a specific time period from the baseline. The drill begins with the player and coach agreeing on the number of quality shots to be hit. This is a player-led drill in which the player decides what constitutes a quality shot and counts out loud every time she thinks she has hit one. This should be interesting information for the coach. The player and coach should come to some agreement on this definition so they can work together on adding more quality shots to the player's game.

VARIATIONS
1. Once the player has reached her goal, the exercise should be repeated with both player and coach counting. This should provide valuable insight into the expectation levels of both parties.
2. The player's practice partner could count instead (or as well). This gives the player valuable feedback from her opponent—a great source of information that is rarely used in tennis.
3. The coach and the players could agree on a number of quality shots to be hit consecutively and on the number of attempts allowed. This drill can be used when working on consistency of all shots—including the serve and return.

COACHING POINTS
The player must realise that a quality shot does not always mean a winning shot. For example, a quality shot may mean scrambling desperately to retrieve a tough drop shot or hitting a high defensive lob into the sun. It may also mean simply touching the ball when under extreme pressure so that the opponent doesn't experience the satisfaction of hitting a clean winner. Everyone will have their own definitions. This is why the drill is so interesting!

DRILL 3.2   Scoring Only With Unforced Errors

This drill rewards consistency in a competitive situation.

AIM
To win with consistency using any game style.

LEVEL
All

DESCRIPTION
In this drill, each player (or doubles team) is allowed to win a point only through an unforced error from the opponent. Normal points are played, but winners and forced errors remain neutral (i.e., there is no change in the score). When there is doubt as to whether an error is forced or unforced, the player who made the error should judge. This is an intriguing exercise because it reveals that players have various definitions of what an unforced error actually is.

VARIATIONS
1. As players improve their ability to build points consistently, they can be allocated one point for a winner or forced error and two points for an opponent's unforced error. This scoring system rewards aggressive play while still punishing unforced errors severely.

2. Players can be allowed a certain number of unforced errors per game, set, or match. Once they reach this threshold, unforced errors start to count as two points against them instead of one.

3. Players can have the chance to increase their threshold of unforced errors by forcing a certain number of forced errors from their opponents. For example, three forced errors can equal one extra unforced error allowed.

COACHING POINTS
This drill teaches players the importance of consistency even when playing with an aggressive, 'first-strike' mentality. It is vital that the coach encourages attacking play at the right moments. Players 'pushing' the ball over the net in fear of error should be punished through the loss of points immediately. As mentioned earlier, players must realise that successful tennis is about maintaining a positive ratio between errors and winners. This scoring system gives the coach the opportunity to balance big differences in playing standards. The coach could, for example, allow a weaker player to win points normally and a stronger player to win points through unforced errors only.

DRILL 3.3   **Playing to a Higher Tempo From the Baseline**

AIM
To learn how to build from the baseline at a higher tempo than normal.

LEVEL
Intermediate to advanced

DESCRIPTION
Players try to achieve a higher rally tempo by agreeing to a certain rally length (e.g., a rally of six) and to hit cooperatively down the middle of the court. When they reach this number, they stop the ball and repeat the drill. Keeping the same length of rally, the players gradually progress to a full-court situation in which both players work at their maximum. The length of rally can be increased as players become more accomplished.

VARIATION
Players can experiment with different ways to start the rally—for example, feed a drive volley, drop shot, short angle slice, aggressive feed down the middle, and so on.

COACHING POINTS
The coach should encourage pace, an aggressive court position, intense movement around the ball, and consistency—all of which require a high level of mental and physical application from both players. Note that this is a cooperative drill, which means that the players must work hard together to achieve their rally target. Winners and errors will inevitably be hit because players try to hit the ball to a higher quality.

DRILL 3.4   Changing the Direction of the Ball From the Baseline

This drill should be used regularly by any aspiring female player because it high-lights many of the qualities required for playing successfully from the baseline.

AIM
To develop an understanding of how and when to change the direction of the ball during an accurate crosscourt baseline rally.

LEVEL
All

DESCRIPTION
Two players (or a coach and a player) rally crosscourt from a hand-feed until one designated player switches the ball down the line and plays the point out. The two should agree to the number of shots that must be hit crosscourt first. For example, a six-shot rally (i.e., three shots each) must be achieved before the designated switcher is allowed to play down the line. Players take turns switching, and the minimum number of crosscourt shots to be hit varies.

VARIATIONS
1. Both players have the chance to switch in the same rally once the cross-court rally total has been achieved.
2. Play progresses from a hand-feed to starting the rally with a serve and return. Take it in turns for the server, then the returner, to have the chance to switch on or after her second shot. The coach should note who is more effective at switching and why.
3. Both the server and the returner have the chance to switch on or after their second shot within the same rally. This variation is very similar to an open point situation, except that the returner must return crosscourt each time.
4. The designated switcher is given the chance to hit down the line with one specific type of shot only. For example, she is allowed to switch with a backhand slice, inside-in forehand, or drop shot. This improves the perception skills of her opponent (she will look out for a change in move-ment or technique) as well as improves the shot selection of the switcher.

COACHING POINTS
The coach should highlight early anticipation of the short ball, fast movement into position, and a safe target area to aim for when switching. Knowing *when* to hit the switch is crucial, and coaches must encourage good shot selection at all times. A player must have enough time to execute her shot, and the switch should be hit from a comfortable position on the court (i.e., not too deep or wide). Also, the coach should emphasise the fact that a player's abil-ity to change the direction of the ball stems directly from the quality of the building shot she hits before it. Therefore, the better the crosscourt shot is, the easier it is to switch down the line.

DRILL 3.5 Running Drives From the Baseline

AIMS
To improve accuracy, consistency, and movement across the baseline.

LEVEL
All

DESCRIPTION
Player A hits only crosscourt, and player B hits only down the line. Player A starts the drill with a hand-feed crosscourt. Both players should be encouraged to work cooperatively. They should have a rally length target to achieve first before a competitive scoring system is introduced. The figure shows the running drives pattern of play.

VARIATIONS
1. Once the running drives pattern has been established, player A can start the rally with a second serve instead of a hand-feed.

2. The coach can experiment with varying competitive scoring systems including greater rewards for the player hitting down the line because she has the more difficult role. (The down-the-line shot is a lower-percentage shot because it is hit over the higher part of the net and into less space.)

3. Instead of hitting down the line every time, player B can hit an agreed number of shots crosscourt first. This can allow both players time to establish a more consistent rhythm before moving across the baseline.

4. Player B is allowed to hit up to three shots crosscourt before hitting down the line. This rule keeps the pattern variable; her opponent must be ready to move across the baseline at any time.

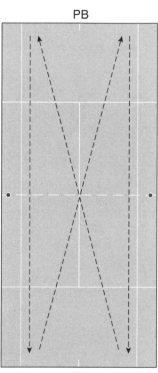

PB

PA

Running drives from the baseline, with one player hitting crosscourt and the other player hitting down the line.

COACHING POINTS
This drill can be difficult to execute consistently because it requires physical endurance, timing, coordination, and concentration. The coach should encourage cooperation, efficient movement, and hitting to high-percentage targets to help both players establish their rhythm.

DRILL 3.6   Baseline Construction

AIMS
To improve accuracy, consistency, concentration, and stamina by building and defending from the baseline.

LEVEL
Intermediate to advanced

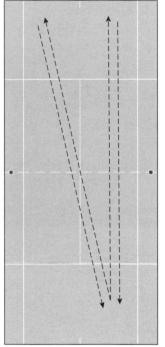

←——— Defender ———→

Constructor

The constructor plays alternate shots from the half court to the defender who covers the whole court.

DESCRIPTION
The constructor (i.e., the player who dictates the play) plays the point out in the half court, while the defender plays in the whole court. The constructor hits crosscourt and down the line alternately, whereas the defender always plays back to the constructor's half of the court. Players play to 11, and the constructor starts the point with a hand-feed crosscourt. The defender is awarded two points to the constructor's one because the defender should always be the underdog to win the point.

VARIATIONS
1. Players keep the same playing pattern and scoring system, but the constructor starts the drill with a hand-feed either crosscourt or down the line. This means that the defender has to be ready to move in either direction immediately.

2. The drill starts with a serve instead of a hand-feed. This means that the defender must return crosscourt, and the server must hit down the line on her second shot. Each player should note how this affects the balance of power. Is the server in more or less control of the point when she starts with a serve instead of a hand-feed?

3. The constructor has a certain number of shots to construct with before the point opens up into the whole court for both players. For example, the constructor is allowed to hit four alternate shots before the defender can hit into the open court. The defender, therefore, has four balls to defend before she can attack into the space. The number of alternate shots allowed can vary from 2 to 10.

4. The constructor can hit alternate forehands from the backhand side of the court (i.e., inside-out and inside-in forehands) to develop the forehand as a weapon.

5. The construction drill is excellent to use when working with three players on court. The constructor always plays on her own, whereas the other two players defend four shots each. The point is played out in the same pattern; each player defends four shots before her partner takes over. The rally often lasts longer because the defender has four shots to recover before playing again. As a result, the constructor usually has to work much harder for her points. Again, the drill can progress to an open court situation, and the number of alternate shots allowed can vary.

COACHING POINTS

The key to the success of this drill is for the constructor to patiently pressure her opponent through accurate and consistent changes of direction. The constructor should look to wear down her opponent rather than try to finish the point immediately. The coach should encourage the constructor to improve movement *around* the ball and the defender to improve movement *to* the ball (because the constructor works in small spaces and the defender moves into big spaces). The coach should also note how long it takes for the constructor to win her points and what type of shots the defender uses when under pressure. The constructor would need to improve the potency of her groundstrokes if she struggles to maintain dominance during the rally, whereas the defender would need to improve accuracy and variety of her defence if she finds it difficult to neutralise effectively.

The defender should be encouraged to use the high and low recovery shot and to experiment by using slice and topspin at different times to see which spin is most effective. Ultimately, the defender's goal is to frustrate the constructor through consistency and tenacity, while the constructor's goal is to gradually break down the defender's physical and psychological resistance.

DRILL 3.7   Counting the Target Hits

This drill is effective when used at the beginning of a practice session as part of a warm-up because it helps to focus a player's mind immediately.

AIMS
To develop depth of shot from the baseline; to develop consistency and concentration.

LEVEL
All

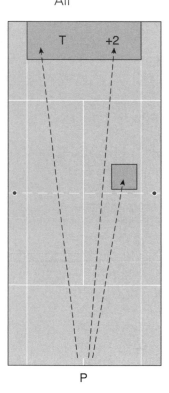

Target areas to aim for to help develop consistency and accuracy.

DESCRIPTION
Nonslip markers form a line across the court about two metres (seven feet) in from the baseline. Each player is given three minutes to hit as many groundstrokes into this target area as possible. The player scores two points when she hits into the target area, zero points for hitting into the court but outside the target area, and minus one point for an error of any type. Coaches should add a short angle target on each side and a drop shot target to encourage variety if desired. In the figure, the player is left-handed, so a drop shot target has been added to encourage her to practice her backhand drop shot down the line. This drill can easily be done with either two or three players. The player not hitting into the target area can keep score.

VARIATIONS
1. The placement of the target area can vary (e.g., the depth target can be placed only halfway across the baseline or along the middle third of the baseline, and the drop shot and short angle targets can also be used).

2. The time allowed to perform the drill can vary, as can the amount of pressure the player is put under.

3. The depth of the target area can vary according to the level of the player, and the scoring system can be adjusted also. For example, players can receive two points for a target hit, one point for a hit into the court but outside the target area, and zero points for any error. (This scoring system is more appropriate for beginners because there is no chance of any minus scores being awarded—thus preventing any negative reinforcement.)

4. Carl Maes (former coach of Kim Clijsters) recommends a slight variation of this drill. Kim would often use this drill as a warm-up for her practice session. Three depth targets are used (+3, +2, and +1) with no score given for any other shot in or out of the court. The player is allowed three minutes to score as many points as possible by hitting down the middle of the court.

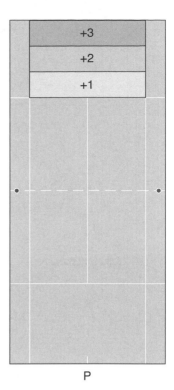

Depth targets used to help develop consistency and accuracy.

COACHING POINTS

Most players comment that when they find their rhythm during this type of drill, they can score very well, hitting many targets consecutively. However, when they miss the target area, they often find it difficult to find their rhythm again quickly enough. A minute can easily go by without them hitting any targets. Therefore, the key to performing this drill successfully is to respond well after missing. This means not allowing an error to affect overall performance. Also, the coach must encourage the player to continue to hit with commitment and aggression when appropriate, because simply floating the ball back into the target area will not improve long-term performance. Finally, as long as a player has physically warmed up thoroughly beforehand, she should be able to hit her first ball with a specific purpose. Often, players and coaches are guilty of allowing too much time for a general tennis warm-up that follows no direction, which uses up valuable practice time. Using the very first ball as part of a drill will help a player understand that *every* ball gives her an opportunity to improve.

DRILL 3.8   Avoiding the Diamond

AIM
To encourage a player to use her creativity by hitting a variety of shots outside the diamond.

LEVEL
All

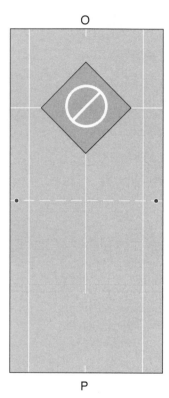

Using the diamond to encourage accuracy and variety of shot.

DESCRIPTION
Nonslip markers are used to create a diamond shape in the centre of the court. Players are not allowed to hit balls into the diamond, whether playing points or practice drills.

COACHING POINTS
The diamond is an excellent shape because it allows for a variety of shots to be hit into the court but outside of the diamond. The diamond itself represents the area of the court that a player's shot would probably least trouble an opponent. Therefore, avoiding this area will help a player outmanoeuvre her opponent more effectively and will help her understand which shots allow her to do this best. The diamond shape allows for short, wide, and deep shots, but punishes the short middle ball. The short angle groundstroke, in particular, can be used to great effect when trying to avoid this area. The size of the diamond should be adjusted to the level of the player. In other words, the better the player is, the bigger the diamond should be.

DRILL 3.9　**The Forbidden Square**

AIM
To encourage a player to use her creativity by hitting a variety of shots outside the square.

LEVEL
All

DESCRIPTION
A player plays normal practice points and drills, but is not allowed to hit into one of the four squares on the court. The forbidden square is agreed on by the player and coach beforehand and can be changed throughout the practice session. Two players can use this drill at once, and each player can have her own forbidden square.

COACHING POINTS
This drill helps to highlight areas of strength, as well as areas that need improvement. It is interesting to note how players use their creativity when their target area is restricted. Often a player has difficulty avoiding one square in particular. For example, a left-handed player with a strong forehand may find it very difficult to play without being able to hit deep crosscourt (player B in the figure). This restriction will force her to use her forehand down the line, her short angle forehand, her backhand crosscourt, and her drop shot more often. Similarly, player A is a right-handed player who struggles to hit her backhand crosscourt groundstroke deep enough. Her forbidden square will force her to hit to a better length on this side.

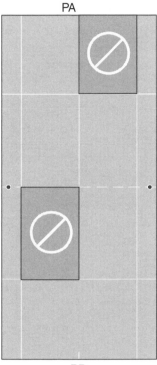

Using the forbidden square to encourage a player's creativity.

DRILL 3.10 Developing the Aggressive Loop

AIMS
To improve depth of shot and variety from the baseline by developing the aggressive loop; to encourage an alternative way to approach the net through good shot selection.

LEVEL
All

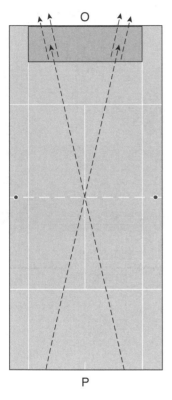

Target area for a player to hit the aggressive loop into.

DESCRIPTION
Nonslip markers are used to form a line across the court about two metres (seven feet) in from the baseline. The player aims to land the ball inside this area with enough spin to force her opponent to hit the ball at or above shoulder height. A player scores a bonus point every time she manages to achieve this within a rally (even if she loses the point), and scores two bonus points if she successfully approaches the net behind the aggressive loop.

COACHING POINTS
The coach should note *when* the player chooses to hit this shot because good shot selection is crucial to its success. Time and space are needed to hit this shot well (as with a topspin lob), along with fast racket head speed that brushes up the back of the ball to create enough pace, spin, and height. The coach should also note whether the player recognises any opportunity to approach or sneak in to the net behind it.

DRILL 3.11 **Playing With 'Space, Not Pace'**

AIM
To encourage the use of variety, including the absorbing slice, by creating spaces on the court without using any pace of shot.

LEVEL
All

DESCRIPTION
Players are not allowed to hit with any pace while playing points. Instead, they are encouraged to win by creating space on the court through the use of angles, high balls, slice shots, drop shots, and so on. Their aim is to hit with as much variety as they can while making their opponent move as much as possible. Bonus points are awarded for special improvisation!

COACHING POINTS
This drill improves variety of shot and feel for the ball and develops a player's awareness of the dimensions of the court. The coach should encourage the use of the absorbing slice and hitting deep down the middle or at a short angle.

DRILL 3.12 **Disguising the Drop Shot**

AIMS
To improve the disguise of the drop shot and to increase awareness of when to play it.

LEVEL
Intermediate to advanced

DESCRIPTION
The coach hand-feeds a ball to the player and instructs her to 'hit' or 'drop' just prior to her forward swing. The coach should progress to basket-feeds and then to open rallies as competency increases and experiment with how early or late the player is given instruction. In an open rally situation the coach must choose to shout 'drop' at the proper time to help educate the player as to *when* to best use the drop shot. The drill can finish with the player simply playing the drop shot within a rally without instruction, trying to disguise it well enough so that the coach cannot anticipate it.

COACHING POINTS
This drill encourages the player to prepare for her groundstroke in the same way as she does for her drop shot—thereby maximising disguise. It increases her general feel for the ball and increases her awareness of when to use the shot. The coach should encourage good shot selection and disguise whenever possible.

DRILL 3.13 Developing Perception Skills

AIM
To develop a player's ability to perceive the oncoming ball quickly and clearly when playing from the baseline.

LEVEL
All

DESCRIPTION
After starting a baseline rally down the middle of the court from a hand-feed, a player is asked to shout a command word as soon as she notices a specific characteristic of the oncoming ball while continuing the rally. She should start by noting the direction of the ball, shouting, 'right', 'left', or 'middle'. Then she should note the height of the ball, shouting, 'high', 'medium', or 'low'.

VARIATIONS
1. Five key characteristics are related to the flight path of the oncoming ball: direction, height, depth, speed, and spin. The player should recognise each one separately and then combine two (e.g., the direction and type of spin of the oncoming ball) as her perception skills develop.

2. The player can experiment by playing with a spin opposite to the one that is played to her; for example, she must hit a slice against her partner's topspin, or vice versa.

3. The player can also be challenged to quickly identify the tactical situation that the oncoming ball puts her in (i.e., build, attack, or defend) or the level of difficulty that she is in (i.e., easy, average, or hard).

COACHING POINTS
Shouting out her perceptions will help direct a player's attention to the oncoming ball immediately. In turn, this will allow for quicker decision making and reaction, helping her maintain the best possible court position for each shot. The coach should note the time difference between the ball being hit and the player's call. He or she should minimise this gap by encouraging the player to anticipate the ball before it is hit (i.e., look for clues by perceiving the position and preparation of the opponent).

DRILL 3.14 **Improving Movement Around the Baseline**

AIM
To improve a player's movement and groundstroke technique when playing from a position in and around the baseline.

LEVEL
Intermediate to advanced

DESCRIPTION
Nonslip markers are put down on the baseline in the shape of a shallow semicircle. Players must play points and baseline drills from inside this area only. Key baseline drills to use with this tool include drill 3.3 ('Playing to a Higher Tempo From the Baseline'), drill 3.4 ('Changing the Direction of the Ball From the Baseline'), and drill 3.6 ('Baseline Construction'). The switcher or constructor must stay inside the area. The defender can play from outside the area if necessary. When playing points, the player can return the first serve from outside the area but must play the remainder of the point from inside. She must play the entire second serve return point from inside also, along with all of her own service points. The depth of the markers can be adjusted according to the competence of the player. Progress the drill to allow both players to move outside this area, providing that they still make *contact* with the ball inside each time.

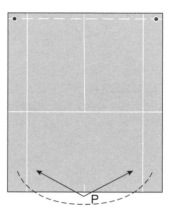

Players must play from inside the semicircle only.

COACHING POINTS
The coach should encourage diagonal movement to the ball as much as possible. Most female players move laterally (side to side) very well but often struggle to move inside the court quickly enough to a short ball. This movement is vital to a player who wants to attack from inside the baseline. Also, the coach should encourage simple, efficient technique because there is less time to prepare for each shot and more pace attached to the oncoming ball from this position.

DRILL 3.15 **Hitting at the Top of the Bounce**

AIMS
To improve the efficiency of a player's technique; to encourage an aggressive court position.

LEVEL
Intermediate to advanced

DESCRIPTION
Starting with a hand-feed, a player tries to hit every ball at the top of its bounce when rallying down the middle of the court from the baseline. She must do this from a wider range of baseline positions as she develops this skill. The drill should progress so that she hits some balls on the rise, some on the drop, and some at the top of the bounce. This will help her develop efficient movement and technique from inside and outside the baseline. Finally, the drill starts with a serve instead of a hand-feed.

COACHING POINTS
This drill has an aim similar to drill 3.14, yet it focuses on the trajectory of the ball instead of on the player's position on court. Once she can execute this technique well enough, the player will naturally play many of her shots from inside the baseline.

DRILL 3.16 **Encouraging an Aggressive Court Position**

AIMS
To develop the ability to play from inside the baseline; to encourage a proactive, first-strike attitude.

LEVEL
Intermediate to advanced

DESCRIPTION
Players play normal points with serve, but as soon as one player is forced to make contact with the ball outside the singles court, her opponent immediately wins the point. In the beginning, one player plays from her normal position and the other plays only from inside the baseline. Players then swap roles and finally progress to both players playing from inside the baseline at the same time.

COACHING POINTS
This is a fun exercise that often pushes a player out of her comfort zone and into the court. It is interesting to note how many shots a player is actually comfortable hitting from inside the baseline and how quickly she adapts her technique. Note also the attitude that each player adopts for this drill. A determination to 'get the first strike in' is crucial if a player is to prevent herself from getting 'knocked out' of the court.

DRILL 3.17 **Finishing the Point With the Shoulder-High Attack**

AIMS
To improve the shoulder-high attack; to learn how to construct an aggressive baseline pattern of play.

LEVEL
Intermediate to advanced

DESCRIPTION
A coach can help develop a player's end game by having her practice the shoulder-high attack first from a series of single-ball feeds. Once the player has developed this skill, the coach can add the most likely shot that will be hit before it, one that forces an opponent to hit a short and high ball. The player should work the point backward from the end game to the start of the point. This exercise helps the player understand how her points are constructed. Consider an example in which a short, shoulder-high, crosscourt forehand is the finishing shot that a player works on developing. The player's shot before the shoulder-high attack is an aggressive inside-out forehand groundstroke. This shot puts the opponent under so much pressure that the player can easily move in and finish with her short forehand. The shot before the inside-out forehand is a deep crosscourt forehand groundstroke that forces a mid-court ball down the middle of the court. This allows the player time to move around her backhand to hit the inside-out forehand. The shot before the deep crosscourt forehand is a first serve hit down the middle from the deuce court. This strong right-handed first serve forces the opponent to contact the ball slightly late on her return, thus setting up the server's deep forehand crosscourt groundstroke. In this way the player has developed a specific four-ball pattern.

VARIATION
The player uses the same drill to set up a number of other end game situations. She can develop the volley, drive volley, and smash as variations of the attacking shots that result from good point construction. Coaches must also emphasise that an attacking shot does not have to be hit as a clean winner; it simply has to increase the pressure put on an opponent.

DRILL 3.18 **Developing the Counterpunch Tactic**

AIM
To develop the counterpunch tactic as a specific way of attacking from the baseline.

LEVEL
Intermediate to advanced

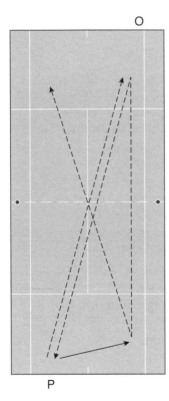

Counterpunching with a right-hander's crosscourt forehand.

DESCRIPTION
A player practices her favourite counterpunch shot from a series of single-ball feeds. This could be a running forehand, a backhand down the line, or a crosscourt passing shot, for example. Once she has developed this shot, she adds the most likely shot that will be hit before it. (This is the same way other end game shots are developed.) For example, if a player's favourite counterpunch shot is a running forehand, then she should develop her backhand crosscourt groundstroke and deliberately hold her position on this side of the court, tempting her opponent to hit down the line to her forehand.

COACHING POINTS
The coach should experiment with a variety of counter-punching shots to see which ones are most effective. He or she should encourage a player to slow down the pace of her groundstrokes to increase the pace later in the rally. The backhand slice is most often used in this way, being hit deep and low crosscourt until an attacking opportunity arises with either a big forehand or an early, aggressive topspin backhand. The short backhand slice can also be used to set up an aggressive counterpunch passing shot or lob. This shot will drag an opponent up the court, forcing her to either play from the net or retreat from a midcourt position. Again, the player should practice the counterpunch shot individually first to build confidence and competence before constructing a pattern around it.

DRILL 3.19 **Defending With Depth**

This drill highlights accuracy, movement, and the ability to defend immediately.

AIM
To improve the depth and consistency of a player's recovery shot.

LEVEL
All

DESCRIPTION
Players rally from a hand-feed; the attacking player covers half of the court and the defending player covers the full court. The defender hits into a designated target area that is positioned in her opponent's half court. The attacker aims to consistently pressure the defender by hitting groundstrokes, played alternately crosscourt and down the line. Once the defender has hit an agreed number of shots into this target area, the point is played out in the full court. For example, the defender may be required to hit two shots into the target area before the point is played out. The defender, therefore, rather than the attacker, dictates when the point is played out.

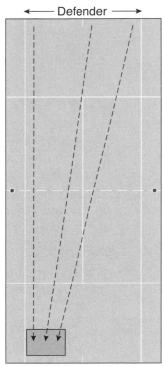

Target area for the defender to hit into before playing out the point.

VARIATIONS
1. The defender agrees to hit a certain number of shots either in a row or in total into her target area (i.e., two shots in a row or two shots in total during the rally). She should progress from a total number to a consecutive number as her level becomes more advanced.

2. The attacker does not have to hit alternate groundstrokes (i.e., crosscourt then down the line consecutively). Instead, she can move the defender around at random, applying pressure on her without trying to hit a winning shot.

3. The number of target hits needed can be increased and the size of the target area decreased as players become more accomplished. Also, the defender can be allowed a certain amount of time or number of shots to reach her agreed number of target hits. If she doesn't reach her goal, the rally is halted.

COACHING POINTS
Coaches must emphasise the importance of hitting into the target area early in the rally because the longer the rally goes on, the harder it becomes for the defender to achieve her desired number of target hits. She becomes physically and mentally fatigued as she covers more ground. This drill reflects the way top-level tennis is being played today. A player will be dominated by her opponent if she doesn't maintain a high quality of shot throughout the rally and if she cannot recover immediately when put under pressure.

DRILL 3.20 **Defending Against the Switch Shot**

AIM
To be able to defend against the switch shot that is played down the line from a crosscourt, baseline rally.

LEVEL
All

DESCRIPTION
Two players rally crosscourt from the baseline. One player (designated beforehand) is allowed to switch down the line at any time. The other player (the defender) has to hit a high-quality recovery shot crosscourt. This recovery shot can be hit deep or short crosscourt, with slice or topspin. The rally then continues crosscourt again until the designated switcher hits down the line once more. Once she plays her second switch down the line, an open point is played out.

VARIATIONS
1. The defender has to hit into a target area on the court after the switcher has hit down the line to continue playing the drill. If she cannot defend into the target, then the rally stops immediately. The size of the target area can be increased or decreased accordingly.
2. The rally continues only if the switcher thinks that the defender has recovered well enough. If the switcher still holds a strong advantage, then she should stop the rally immediately. This provides valuable instant feedback to the defender about the quality of her recovery shots.
3. The number of switch balls hit before an open point is played out can be increased or decreased.

COACHING POINTS
The coach should note how well the defender deals with her opponent's switch shot. Is she able to neutralise the threat of the switch, or is the switcher in control of the point? From which side does the defender recover best? Is a slice or topspin recovery shot more effective? Finally, the coach should make sure that the short slice crosscourt ball stays low enough and that the topspin shot has enough spin to pull the attacking player short and wide. Experimenting with these different defensive options will help a player to understand exactly how she defends most effectively.

DRILL 3.21 **Using the Two-Ball Defence**

AIM
To improve a player's ability to defend effectively and immediately from the baseline.

LEVEL
All

DESCRIPTION
One player is the designated attacker, and the other player is the designated defender. The coach feeds a midcourt ball for the aggressor to attack. She is allowed two shots (including the coach's feed) to attack with. The defender must be able to neutralise the rally within the first two shots; otherwise, the rally is stopped. If she manages to neutralise, then the point is played out in the whole court.

VARIATIONS
1. Players hit the first four balls (the two aggressive shots and the two defensive shots) down the middle of the court. This gives each player the chance to improve technique without having to cover the whole court. (Alternatively, players could rally crosscourt instead of down the middle.)

2. The attacker must hit both balls to a designated half of the court, whereas the defender is allowed to hit into the whole court.

3. The point is played out, but the defender is awarded two points if she manages to win by neutralising quickly.

4. As players become more accomplished, the number of defensive shots allowed can be reduced (i.e., the defender must neutralise immediately). Coaches can also experiment with the depth, height, and width of their feeds.

COACHING POINTS
The coach should note the type of shots that are used to defend with and from which side each player defends more effectively. Players should have quick perception of the oncoming ball, with fast, balanced movement and simple technique on recovery shots. They should use a mix of high and low recovery shots based on whether or not the attacking player is approaching the net.

DRILL 3.22 **Defending as a Team in Doubles**

AIMS
To improve a doubles pair's ability to defend as a team; to develop communication and court awareness.

LEVEL
All

DESCRIPTION
The coach hand-feeds a ball to an attacking pair that is positioned at the net. The defending pair is positioned on the baseline. The teams play the point out from this situation and switch roles when one pair wins to 11 points. The coach should vary the type and difficulty of feeds, sometimes feeding an easy smash and then a tough volley, and so on.

VARIATIONS
1. The defending pair stays on the baseline, but the formation of the attacking pair changes to either one-up/one-back, or both back.
2. The defending pair is allowed to hit only specific shots from the baseline (e.g., they may hit only one lob during the rally, they must hit only lobs during the rally, or they must hit a volley by their third shot).

COACHING POINTS
The coach should encourage clear and positive communication between partners and make sure both players work together as one unit—that is, moving up, back, and sideways in parallel. What types of shots are being used to defend with? How creative are the players in changing a defensive situation into an attacking one? The coach should also note how the attacking team copes with having no definite volley targets to aim for when its opponents are both back.

DRILL 3.23 **Defending Against the Drop Shot**

AIMS
To improve a player's ability to defend against the drop shot; to increase a player's anticipation and perception skills; to develop efficient movement up the court.

LEVEL
All

DESCRIPTION
The coach feeds a series of three drop shots in a row to the player, who returns to the baseline after retrieving each one. The coach feeds from the midcourt (to help accuracy) and either follows the drop shot in to the net or moves back to the baseline. The player must move to the drop shot as quickly as possible and choose the right type of defence depending on the coach's position and the amount of pressure she is under.

VARIATION
The coach feeds one of the balls deep instead of short to encourage quick perception of the flight path of the ball. The coach starts the drill by not disguising the deep ball, allowing the player the chance to anticipate it. As the player progresses, the coach disguises the feeds to make each shot harder to read.

COACHING POINTS
The coach should encourage fast movement straight to the ball. He or she should make sure the player returns to a balanced ready position before feeding the next ball and look for how early she anticipates and perceives this next ball. The coach should encourage good shot selection based on each playing situation.

Playing the Net

emale players are choosing to approach and play at the net more carefully because the strength of the passing shot and lob has improved so much in recent years. Opponents are moving faster and hitting harder and often enjoy having a player at the net to aim past. Also, the opportunities to play from the net are less apparent because so many players hit more aggressively from the baseline. As a result, the traditional ways of approaching the net (e.g., the serve and volley, the chip and charge, and the down-the-line approach) are being used less often. Instead, many players now prefer to build and attack from the baseline before finishing the point with a single volley, or smash, at the net. In other words, much of the work in creating an advantage is done before a volley is played. This more selective approach to playing at the net has meant that female players are often more effective at the net than are their male counterparts.

Table 4.1 shows the percentage of points won at the net by male and female players at the four Grand Slams in 2001. On each occasion, female players won relatively more points at the net than male players did. Given that women approach the net less often than men, these statistics suggest that the female player picks her moment to approach the net more carefully—and uses the volley as a finish shot rather than a building shot. Male players, on the other hand, tend to approach the net more often and are prepared to take more risk when doing so.

Female players now use two contrasting ways of approaching the net. The *instinctual* approach means a player decides to come in after seeing the effectiveness of her previous shot, whereas the *planned* approach means that she decides to come in before hitting her shot—no matter what the outcome. This chapter studies these two methods of approaching the net along with the shots that are used at the net, including the drive volley, sneak volley, short angle volley, and smash. It also discusses the need for anticipation, correct court positioning, and instinctual and planned interception (in doubles).

Table 4.1 Percentage of Points Won at the Net When Serving and Returning

Player	Sex	Australian	French	Wimbledon	US Open
Server	F	64.6 %	67.8 %	65.6 %	64.4 %
Server	M	60.6 %	64.5 %	58.1 %	61.4 %
Returner	F	68.0 %	68.4 %	71.8 %	67.2 %
Returner	M	59.9 %	63.5 %	58.3 %	61.8 %

Adapted from P. O'Donoghue and B. Ingram, 2001, "A notational analysis of elite tennis strategy" *Journal of Sports Sciences* 19(2): 107-115, by permission of Taylor & Francis Ltd. http://www.tandf.co.uk/journals.

Instinctual Net Play

The majority of players on the WTA Tour use the instinctual approach to access the net. In other words, they wait to see the effectiveness of their baseline shot before deciding to approach the net at the last moment. When a player uses this tactic, her shot gives her opponent no clue as to whether she will be approaching the net. Therefore, her opponent does not know whether to hit a passing shot or not. It is this surprise element that proves so valuable. This tactic allows a player to pick and choose her net play points very carefully, providing her with the best possible chance of success as a result. A player's decision to play from the net will be based mainly on her opponent's court position and her likely next shot. If she perceives her opponent to be in a defensive position, she may start to move forward in anticipation of an easy ball to volley against. She will fully commit to approaching the net once she perceives the actual flight path of her opponent's shot. This instinctual tactic allows the player the option of staying on the baseline if the opponent defends very effectively.

The key to using the instinctual approach lies in a player's ability to anticipate her opponent's next shot. Understanding when her opponent is likely to defend—and moving forward accordingly—will give her the best chance of playing the oncoming ball out of the air. Being able to quickly perceive the flight path of this ball is important also because ultimately, this will determine whether she volleys it (depending on how easy it is). Any delay in making this decision will often result in a missed opportunity.

The two shots that are most commonly used with this tactic are the drive volley and the sneak volley. Each shot is described in detail in the following sections.

Drive Volley

The drive volley has become a crucial shot in women's tennis because it provides a valuable link between the baseline and the net. It is used when a player moves inside the baseline to hit her opponent's high, floating defensive shot out of the air without bouncing, allowing the opponent little time to prepare. Crucially, it is hit using groundstroke technique (i.e., a fast swing brushing up the back of the ball that generates topspin, as opposed to a traditional block). Because this shot makes use of the familiar groundstroke technique, it is an excellent way of introducing net play to players who lack confidence coming forward.

The drive volley is hit with aggression from anywhere inside the court, but does not require an immediate commitment to follow it in to the net. Most players will hit the drive volley into big target areas (because it is hit with much power and spin) and will only decide to approach the net after they have perceived its effectiveness. Most drive volleys are hit from between the baseline and the service line, allowing a player the option of quickly returning to the baseline if she feels that her opponent has not been put under enough pressure. Very often, the point is won because of the pace and spin of the ball overpowering an opponent. Otherwise, it can leave a simple volley, smash, or short groundstroke to win the point with.

Practicing the drive volley will naturally improve a player's groundstroke technique (shoulder-high attack shots in particular), and more importantly, will help her maintain control over an opponent who uses the high recovery shot to defend with (see chapter 3). The key to its success lies in a player's ability to recognise this high ball quickly enough. Some less experienced players do not recognise a drive volley opportunity until it is too late, which usually results in their allowing the ball to bounce and giving their opponent too much time to recover.

To practice the drive volley, see drill 4.1 on page 148.

Sneak Volley

Sam's exceptional doubles skills have really helped her singles game. She enjoys playing at the net and uses a mixture of sneak and planned approaches to get her there.

—Craig Morris, Tennis Australia Coach Education Manager and former coach to Sam Stosur, Number 1 Doubles and Top 30 Singles Player in 2006

Used in a similar way to the drive volley, the sneak volley (or ghost volley) is played when a player reacts quickly to her opponent's defensive position. The sneak volley is not a planned shot; rather, it is played instinctively once a short or floating ball has been perceived. A player moves in swiftly to volley this ball before allowing her opponent time to recover. This type of volley will usually be hit against a defensive shot that stays fairly low, as opposed to the drive volley, which is usually hit against a higher, defensive ball. The sneak volley is hit as a traditional 'punch' volley because placement and control is required rather than power.

The sneak volley tactic requires early anticipation of the opponent's defensive position, quick perception of the flight path of the ball, and fast movement forward to the net. These skills are crucial because this volley is usually hit closer to the net than the drive volley. This is because the ball travels at a lower height, requiring the player to contact it earlier in its flight path before it drops too low to volley against. The point is won by applying time pressure on an opponent and placing the volley accurately.

To practice the sneak volley tactic, see drill 4.2 on page 149.

Planned Net Play

Planned net play differs from instinctual net play in that the player decides to approach the net before she hits her next shot. This means that she comes in using a specific approach shot to create an opportunity to win the point with a volley or smash. This planned tactic allows the player to close in tightly on the net because there is no delay while she waits to see the effectiveness of her approach. Also, closing in on the net reduces the space available for an opponent to hit her passing shot into. However, this tactic carries more risk because the player commits herself to approaching—even if her approach shot is less than effective! Therefore, how and where a player approaches to is important along with her choice of volley or smash once at the net.

Approach Shot

Two types of planned approach shots can help a player establish a dominant net position: the short angle approach and the down-the-line approach. Both of these shots attempt to pressure an opponent through accurate placement and spin. They are usually hit with slice, meaning that the ball stays low and is difficult for an opponent to attack because she is forced to hit the ball up over the net. These two shots allow a player to establish a strong net position before using the volley or smash to win the point.

The short angle approach is effective because it forces an opponent to move forward to a short, wide ball. This movement pattern often creates difficulty for an opponent and can force her into a defensive position because she must play from an unfamiliar court position. It is important to note that it is harder for a player to create a short angle approach from the middle of the court because there are fewer angles available. Therefore, most angled approaches are hit from wider positions. The slice approach, in particular, gives an opponent trouble because the ball stays short and low, preventing her from being able to get 'under' the ball. A player can then afford to close in on the net quite tightly and be ready to volley because the opponent is unlikely to be able to hit an aggressive lob over her. Moving closer in reduces the space available for the pass and can also intimidate an opponent into making an error. Another way of approaching with a short angle is by hitting a 'whipped' topspin, short angle groundstroke. This is often played when the player has moved well inside the baseline because she senses a short ball or volley. The player uses very fast racket head speed to create the topspin needed to 'kick' the ball short and wide of the court. This shot can 'drag' an opponent off the court, leaving a simple volley to finish the point with. Figure 4.1 shows the target areas for the short angle approach. Note also how an opponent is dragged wide of the court, allowing the player to approach the net and finish the point with a volley, hit into the open court.

The down-the-line approach shot is a groundstroke hit from inside the baseline that a player uses to follow in to the net with. It is usually hit with slice (so that the ball stays low and is harder to attack) and to a deep, accurate line target. This shot will prove most effective on fast courts (where the ball bounces fast and low) and against opponents with extreme grips (making it hard for them to hit 'under' the ball). Most important, it prevents a natural space from opening up for the opponent to hit her passing shot into. After the approach, the net player prepares to volley by covering the line and middle of the court more than the wide, crosscourt space. This is because the more pressure the opponent is under, the less likely she is to make the passing shot crosscourt because she has to create this space herself. A slight alternative to this shot is the deep, middle approach. Again, this shot prevents an opponent from using any natural angles, forcing her to create a space. Figure 4.2 shows the area of the net a player should cover when she

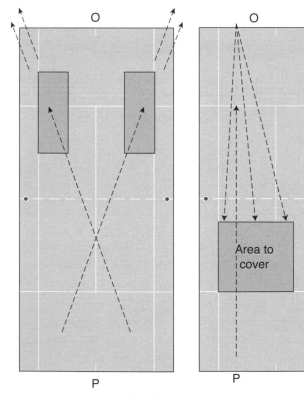

FIGURE 4.1   **Target areas used for the short angle approach.**

FIGURE 4.2   **Area of the net to cover having approached deep down the line.**

approaches down the line. This right-handed net player has approached down the line behind her backhand slice. The shaded area indicates the most likely direction of her opponent's passing shot or lob.

To practice the tactics discussed in this section, see drill 4.3 on page 150.

Volley

I encourage the intercept volley as much as possible. The volleyer has to be willing to take a chance, to possibly look foolish, and to perhaps lose the point—but the payoff is that she will get a lot of free points because her opponents will be watching out for her for the rest of the match.

—Amy Jensen, Three-Time NCAA Doubles Champion

A player's ability to volley effectively at the net will depend very much on the quality of her approach shot, because this shot creates a net play situation. However, where she chooses to volley, once at the net, remains a key factor also because this will directly affect the passing shot and lob options for her opponent. In most cases, the placement and accuracy of the volley are the most crucial aspects because this shot is hit with control rather than power (the volley requires a short, blocking action rather than a long swinging action). The placement of the volley assumes even greater importance as a player is put under more pressure at the net because it is more difficult for her to apply any other qualities to the ball (such as pace or spin). Similar to the approach shot, there are two key volleys that should be used as much as possible: the short angle volley and deep-down-the-line volley. When each one of these shots is played depends very much on the tactical position of the net player.

Net players are frequently choosing to use the short angle volley because it prevents an opponent from moving laterally and forces her to move diagonally toward the ball instead. This is because it is hit into a short and wide area of the court (toward the side of each service box) with a lot of control but without much pace. This placement usually results in an opponent moving in *two* different directions to hit the passing shot or lob, rather than one. This can result in a more defensive shot being played because by the time the opponent has reached this dropping ball, she has to hit it *up* over the net. Opponents tend to find a diagonal movement pattern harder, usually because they perceive the direction of the ball before they perceive the depth of the ball (i.e., two-dimensional perception occurs before three-dimensional perception). Aside from the difficulty in perceiving the short angle volley, some suggest that players struggle with this movement because they are taught at a very early age to 'turn and hit' when they are hand-fed the ball. This initial turn can prevent quick movement to the short ball because the player is forced to hop forward (from a sideways stance). The short angle volley should only be played when the net player is in good control of her shot. This volley requires accurate placement of the ball (short and wide) and an ability to take pace off the oncoming ball to keep it from bouncing too deep toward the opponent. In other words, feel and composure on the ball are crucial.

The short angle volley is often preferred to the deep angle volley because the deep angle volley requires an opponent to move in only one direction—that is, laterally across the baseline. The placement of this volley often is easier to return as a result. Figures 4.3 and 4.4 show the effectiveness of both types of volleys. In figure 4.3 the player approaching the net has hit a deep angle volley crosscourt to a right-handed opponent's forehand side. Her opponent has moved comfortably across the baseline (strong lateral movement) to hit an aggressive passing shot or lob. This is simple for her because she has had to move in only one direction toward the ball. In figure 4.4 the player approaching the net has hit a short angle volley crosscourt. In this situation, the opponent instinctively moves across the baseline before perceiving the depth of the oncoming ball. When she realises that the ball is short, she has to change her line of movement to move up the court.

When a player is under pressure at the net, she may choose to hit her volley deeper rather than attempting to hit a short angle that may prove more difficult for her to execute. In this case, it is often more effective for a player to use the volley down the line, rather than the volley crosscourt. Playing down the line prevents an opponent from running laterally onto the ball and hitting into any natural space. This contrasts with the deep volley crosscourt that opens up a space for a passing shot to be hit down the line. In other words, the down-the-line volley forces an opponent to create her own space and possibly make an error as a result. Figure 4.5 shows the differences in effectiveness of these two volleys. In this example, the deep volley down the line forces the opponent to create a crosscourt angle in order to pass the net player, whereas the deep crosscourt volley creates a natural space for an opponent to hit into.

When a net player is under pressure, the deep volley, hit down the line or middle, is preferable to a short angle volley. The short angle volley needs to be hit with a high degree of control and feel because it requires a player to absorb the pace of the oncoming ball and hit it back to an accurate target area. This shot is harder to execute when a net player

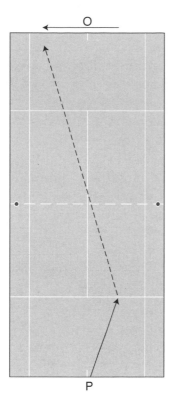

FIGURE 4.3 **Playing the deep angle volley, which allows an opponent one line of movement to the ball.**

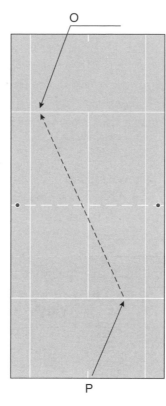

FIGURE 4.4 **Playing the short angle volley, which forces an opponent to move in two different directions.**

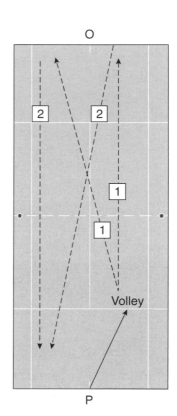

FIGURE 4.5 **Options available to an opponent in response to a deep-down-the-line volley compared to a deep crosscourt volley.**

is under real pressure. If the short angle volley doesn't stay short, low, or wide enough, then it becomes an easy ball for an opponent to pass with. However, sometimes a volleyer is under such extreme pressure by an aggressive passing shot that her first goal is to simply get the ball back over the net! Sometimes, just getting a racket on the ball to produce a short volley will actually be enough to win the point—especially against the aggressive passing shot down the line. This may be because the baseline player is not expecting the ball to come back, or because she simply doesn't move up the court very well. Whatever the reason, players must be encouraged to touch with their racket every ball that passes them. In this way they at least deny their opponent the feeling of hitting a clean winner!

To practice volley tactics, see drill 4.4 on page 151.

Smash

The smash is played against a ball that travels over and above the head of the net player. It is hit using serve technique and therefore requires precise positioning underneath the ball. This is because the required swing is longer and requires more coordination than the swing needed for a volley (the same reason that a server must toss the ball accurately). This longer swing allows the player to impart more power and spin on the ball.

Having a strong and reliable smash is a great advantage to a female player. Unlike in the men's game (where having a powerful smash is almost a prerequisite), not all women hit this shot to a high enough quality. This contrast in execution is attributable to the difference in height and upper-body strength between male and female players. Many female players try to win all their points from the baseline because they are fearful of playing from the net. This mentality often leads to a player forcing her shots too much from the back of the court and making too many errors as a consequence. Although executing the smash can be difficult for females, this shot is often under estimated and certainly not practiced enough, even though it should be included as an important part of a player's attacking options.

The smash should be used when the oncoming ball travels too high for the player to hit as a volley. This is generally around head height and above. Similar to the drive volley, the smash should be hit into big target areas on the court because its power, rather than its placement, usually overwhelms an opponent, and also because an opponent often chooses a side to defend after lobbing—and moves there *before* the smash is hit. Areas such as the middle T on the court can provide excellent high-percentage targets to aim for when an opponent moves too early.

© Icon Sports Media

A strong smash should be aimed well inside the lines of the court.

The smash (and bounce smash) should be practiced from all areas of the court. Sometimes, however, a player can have difficulty deciding whether to smash, drive volley, or volley a ball because the trajectory of the oncoming ball (i.e., its height, spin, and depth) is hard to read. Early perception and decision making are vital in this situation because each shot requires different technique and different positioning.

Drills 4.5 and 4.6 on pages 152 to 153 can help a player improve her technique and confidence on the smash, and drills 4.7 and 4.8 on pages 154 to 155 can help her develop winning combinations with the volley and smash at the net.

Coaching Tip

To encourage smart net play, the coach should award two bonus points when a rally is won with a drive volley, volley, or smash. He or she should award one bonus point if a drive volley, volley, or smash has been played within a winning rally. Equally, points should be subtracted when a player misses an opportunity to approach the net. This is an important point. Players must learn to take their opportunities instantly because they may not get another chance within the rally—especially when playing at a high level.

One of the most common formations in women's doubles (especially with younger players) is the one-player-up/one-player-back position. This position occurs after the serve and return have been played and a neutral crosscourt rally between the two opposing baseline players has begun. This formation is most often used between opposing pairs who choose to serve and stay back rather than use the serve and volley tactic. There are two key tactical intentions when playing from this position: the net player looks to intercept with a winning volley and the baseline player looks to approach the net.

The better the crosscourt groundstroke played by the baseline partner is, the more chance the net partner has of intercepting with a volley. Generally, the wider the groundstroke is, the more chance the net player has of intercepting the opponent's reply. This is because it is harder for an opponent to keep the ball away from the net player from a wide baseline position than from a middle position. The net player moves forward to the ball she is about to volley. This movement allows her to play the shot more aggressively. She should hit it into the intercept volley target area, which is positioned in the middle of the court. This allows for a high margin of error. It also results in the volley being hit down to the feet of, or behind, an opposing net player, which is very difficult to defend against. In figure 4.6 a crosscourt groundstroke rally has been played, and the net player uses the intercept volley to win the point. Note how the opposing baseline player hasn't been able to create enough angle cross-court to hit past the net player. The net player must cover the down-the-line groundstroke from this wide position also (similar to covering the line after a wide serve). An opponent will often play down the line from a wide baseline position, especially if she sees the net player anticipating the intercept volley by moving across the net too early. Drill 4.9 on page 156 will help to highlight when to use the intercept volley and will allow a doubles pair to play more effectively as a team.

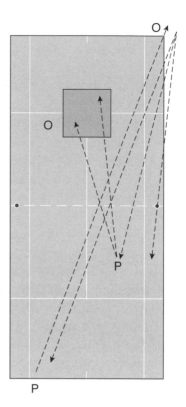

FIGURE 4.6 Using the intercept volley after a wide, building crosscourt groundstroke.

The second main tactical objective from a one-up/one-back formation is for the baseline player to join her partner at the net. The baseline player can use a variety of shots to approach with, just as she can in singles. These could include the deep slice approach (crosscourt to the opposing baseline player), the short angle topspin or slice approach (used to drag the opponent short and wide), the building crosscourt groundstroke, the aggressive loop, and the drop shot. Once both players are at the net, they must form a strong team—moving forward, sideways, and backward together as one unit; communicating clearly; assigning responsibilities (e.g., who takes the lob down the middle?); and making correct shot selections.

Choosing the direction of the volley and smash, in particular, is crucial when both players are playing at the net. A key rule is for them to play down the *middle* of the court when under pressure (see figure 4.7) and to play *wide* of the court when in an attacking position (see figure 4.8). The volley (and smash) hit down the middle reduces the angles available to an opposing team and gives the net pair the chance to maintain control over the centre of the net. The volley (and smash) hit wide is a better option for the net pair when in a dominant position because once their opponents are wide of the court, they will have created more space to hit into (which will help them finish the point).

To practice the tactics discussed in this section, see drills 4.9 and 4.10 on pages 156 and 157.

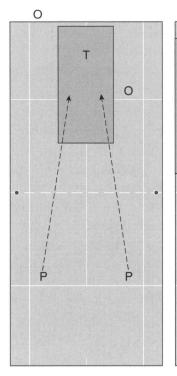

FIGURE 4.7 The volley and smash target area for the doubles team that is under pressure at the net.

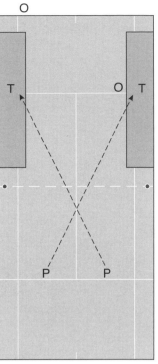

FIGURE 4.8 The volley and smash target areas for the doubles team that is in a dominant position at the net.

Standing Ground at the Net

Sometimes a player hasn't put her opponent under enough pressure when approaching the net. In this case she will often feel like a 'sitting duck', an easy target for her opponent to hit past (or at!). As a result, the net player will often guess which side the passing shot will be hit to and move there before the shot has been played. If she makes this movement too early, her opponent will simply hit her passing shot into the space she has left. In other words, she has made her opponent's decision as to where to hit! It can be more effective, therefore, for the player to *hold* her position at the net, standing her ground until the opponent actually hits the ball. This tactic forces her opponent to make the decision as to which side to hit to. This can distract an opponent who is waiting for the net player to make the first move. When the net player doesn't make a move, the opponent has to make a last-minute decision that can affect the execution of her passing shot or lob. This tactic could be used whenever the net player is unsure of where her opponent will hit to.

To practice standing ground at the net, see drill 4.11 on page 158.

The importance of standing ground at the net, especially when under pressure, applies equally to a doubles team. The net players must try to hold their positions together rather than move in different directions, because this will prevent any significant spaces from opening up between them. Reducing the space available for an opposing team is a key tactic in doubles. Doing this effectively can easily result in an opposing pair forcing its shots too much. Also, standing ground at the net as a team sends a strong psychological message that both players are prepared to stand together in battle! This is an important point. Doing this well in the early stages of a match shows teamwork and togetherness and can often force an opposing team into trying to play *too* well in order to win.

To practice defending the net as a doubles team, see drill 4.12 on page 159.

Using Anticipation at the Net

When a player approaches and plays from the net, she can predict what an opponent will do—or what she is likely *not* to do—by using tactical and technical anticipation. This means studying the previous playing habits and stroke technique of her opponent, as well as using her own past playing experiences to understand which shots her opponent is most likely to hit.

For example, an opponent will likely only be able to pass down the line (or middle) when the ball is beating her for pace and width. This is because it is difficult for her to contact the ball early enough to create a crosscourt angle. As a result, the net player will cover the line and middle of the court more when coming in. She will also move closer to the net as more pressure is applied, because there is less chance of her opponent hitting an offensive lob. In this case, the player is using her previous tennis experiences to help her understand the tactical options available to her opponent. The same principle applies to the drop shot and short angle approach, when the opponent is obviously struggling to move forward quickly enough. The net player, using tactical anticipation, will close in and offer her opponent little space to hit into because she knows that her opponent can only hit up, and probably short, over the net.

Similarly, by studying an opponent's movement and stroke technique, the player can gain clues as to which shot she will play next. For example, seeing a double-handed player take one hand off the racket to reach a wide ball is a good indicator of a defensive shot. In the same way, seeing an opponent lean back in an open stance with her racket head dropped very low will help the player to anticipate a lob.

Anticipation will help the player move in and around the net more effectively also. Female players who are unfamiliar with playing at the net will often move sideways too early when approaching, to cover the middle of the court. As a result, they will often lose out on gaining valuable forward ground and leave too much space open for the down-the-line passing shot in particular. It is important for them to realise that they don't always have to position themselves centrally, because their position depends greatly on the type of approach played and the position of their opponent.

To practice the tactics discussed in this section, see drill 4.13 on page 160.

Summary

- [ ] Because the strength of the passing shot and lob has increased so much in recent years, female players are now using a wide variety of ways to approach and play from the net. They are using the instinctual approach, in particular, which requires a player to choose to come in after she has seen the effectiveness of her previous shot. This contrasts with the more traditional, planned approach, which requires a player to choose to come in before she hits her next shot.

- [ ] The drive volley plays a crucial role in women's tennis because it provides a valuable link between the baseline and the net. It is played using groundstroke technique and is best hit out of the air against a high, floating ball. It can be hit into big target areas because it carries much pace and spin, allowing an opponent very little time to defend against it. The key to its success lies in a player's ability to recognise when to play it quickly enough.

- [ ] The sneak volley is played instinctively once a player has perceived a short or floating ball. This shot will be hit against a lower defensive ball, compared to the drive volley, which is hit against a higher one. The sneak volley requires a player to anticipate her opponent's defensive position, perceive the flight path of the oncoming ball, and move quickly in to the net. Again, time pressure is applied to an opponent as long as the volley is played with accuracy and control.

☐ The short angle approach has the same effect as the short angle volley because it forces an opponent to move forward to a short, wide ball. The slice approach will stay low and will prevent an opponent from being able to hit under the ball. The topspin approach will drag an opponent off the court and will create a natural space for the volley or smash to be hit into.

☐ The approach shot, hit deep down the line or middle, is used to great effect by the player who has a strong backhand slice. Most important, just like the down-the-line volley, it prevents a natural space from opening up.

☐ The short angle volley is frequently used today because it forces an opponent to move across and up the court in a diagonal direction. This often results in an opponent moving in two directions (sideways, then forward), increasing the time it takes her to reach the ball. When volleying for depth, a player will be more effective volleying down the line or middle of the court because these two shots force an opponent to create a space to hit into, compared to the crosscourt volley that opens up a natural space.

☐ The smash can be hit into big target areas on the court because its power, rather than its placement, usually overwhelms an opponent. In most cases, playing confidently at the net will allow a player to play with less pressure from the baseline.

☐ In doubles, a primary tactical objective for the net player is to look to intercept with a winning volley, when playing in a one-up/one-back formation. Generally, the wider the crosscourt groundstroke is, the more chance the net player has of intercepting. It is equally important, however, for the net player to cover her line from this wide position, because an opponent on the baseline will look to hit here if she sees the net player moving across the net too quickly.

☐ Another key tactic, when playing in this doubles formation, is for the baseline player to join her partner at the net. Once both players are at the net, they must form a strong team. This includes moving together as one unit, assigning responsibilities, and communicating clearly and efficiently.

- [ ] Choosing where to volley and smash to is crucial when both players are playing at the net as a doubles team. A key rule is for them to play down the middle of the court when under pressure and to play wide of the court when in an attacking position.

- [ ] A player should stand her ground when under pressure at the net rather than decide to cover one side of the court too early. This tactic forces her opponent to make the decision as to which side to hit to. The same holds true for the players in a doubles pair, who must ensure that they hold their positions together at the net (preventing any space from opening up between them).

- [ ] A player can predict what an opponent will do—or what she is likely *not* to do—by using tactical and technical anticipation. This involves studying the previous playing habits and stroke technique of her opponent, as well as using her own past playing experiences to understand which shots her opponent is most likely to hit.

DRILL 4.1   Using the Drive Volley to Attack

AIMS
To improve a player's drive volley technique; to help her recognise when to play it, what to do after it, and how to perceive its effectiveness.

LEVEL
All

DESCRIPTION
The drill starts with single-ball feeds. A player hits the drive volley with fast racket head speed and aggression into big targets placed well inside the baseline. As the player becomes more proficient at this shot, the coach and player play the point out after the drive volley has been hit. The coach deliberately plays defensively after the drive volley (to encourage the player to approach the net) or aggressively (to see whether she moves back to the baseline quickly enough). The coach and the player should discuss the choices the player made after seeing the effectiveness of her drive volley. The drill progresses to an open rally situation in which the coach deliberately plays a high, floating ball when under pressure. The coach should note how quickly (if at all) the player recognises this ball as a drive volley opportunity and should play the point out accordingly. Again, the coach and the player should discuss the tactical choices made after hitting it.

COACHING POINTS
The player should be encouraged to hit the drive volley from both her fore-hand and backhand sides. Which side does she create more pace or angle with? Does this mirror how she uses her groundstrokes? Is she comfortable moving in behind both shots? The coach should remind her that she can afford to hit this shot with a high margin of error because the pace and spin that she uses is often enough to overpower an opponent. Also, she should practice hitting the drive volley from a lower ball. This helps to develop smooth and coordinated technique because the wrist, arm, and shoulder must swing the racket loosely to generate the necessary spin.

DRILL 4.2   **Developing the Sneak Volley**

AIMS
To improve a player's execution of the sneak volley; to develop an understanding of when to play the sneak volley.

LEVEL
Intermediate to advanced

DESCRIPTION
The drill starts with a single-ball feed. The player starts moving in to the net just before the coach hits the ball (i.e., as the ball bounces before the coach's feed). Short angle and deep line targets are placed on the court for the player to aim for. The player moves in and volleys each ball to either the short angle or deep line target, depending on the difficulty of the feed. An easy ball should be hit to the short angle target, whereas a more difficult one should be hit down the line. As the player develops this shot, the drill progresses to a two-ball feed (i.e., the player hits two shots instead of one); the player has to hit a building groundstroke before moving in to hit the volley.

VARIATION
The player must hit the sneak volley as soon as the coach hits a defensive shot. The player may agree beforehand with the coach which shot she will sneak in against. For example, she may agree to use the sneak volley when a double-handed player is forced to hit a single-handed shot (because she is under pressure). She gains a bonus point when she sees the sneak opportunity early enough and is penalised a point when she misses a chance to come in. The coach should note how quickly she perceives this defensive ball and how fast she moves in to the net. This condition will help to develop her anticipation and perception skills, as well as her movement toward the net.

COACHING POINTS
The coach should encourage the player to anticipate the opponent's playing position. Is the opponent likely to hit a defensive shot based on her court position? Is she likely to slice the ball based on her backswing? Is her defensive shot likely to go down the line based on her contact point? The player should learn to perceive the flight path of the ball quickly. One way to do this is to shout 'high', 'middle', or 'low' as soon as she sees the ball. She should also try to make contact with the ball from inside the service line. This will develop faster movement forward and will take valuable time away from an opponent.

DRILL 4.3 **Developing a Planned Approach Shot**

AIMS
To develop a planned approach shot; to understand how and when to use a planned approach shot.

LEVEL
All

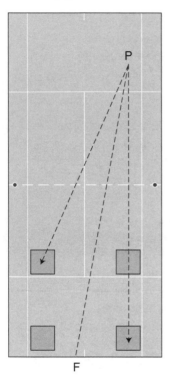

The deep-down-the-line target and short angle target for the forehand and backhand approach shot.

DESCRIPTION
A short angle target and a deep line target are placed on the court. The coach starts the drill by giving the player single-ball feeds to her backhand side and asking her to hit alternate approach shots to the two targets. The player must experiment by trying to hit either slice or topspin to both targets. As her approach shots develop, the coach feeds a second ball for the player to volley after she hits the initial approach shot. This feed should be relative to the quality of the player's approach shot. Therefore, if her short angle approach stays wide and low, she should receive a high, floating ball to volley away. If her approach is not hit to a high enough quality, then she should have to play a tougher volley. The drill is also reversed to allow the player the chance to experiment with the forehand approach.

VARIATION
The drill progresses to playing the point out from the coach's hand-feed, and the player has to approach to either target immediately. This is followed by adding the serve and return and allocating bonus points for correct shot selections (i.e., did the player choose the correct ball to come in on? Did she hit to an appropriate target? Did she cover the correct area at the net?).

COACHING POINTS
The coach should note whether the player is more effective from her forehand or backhand side, whether she prefers hitting to the short angle or deep line target, and whether she is better using the slice or topspin approach. Also, when does she choose to approach? Does she recognise realistic net play opportunities? The coach should encourage a small split-step before her approach shot and volley with smooth, balanced movement to the net. The player should hit the opposite volley to her approach; that is, if approaching deep down the line, she should hit a short angle volley so that an opponent has the maximum court distance to cover between shots, and vice versa.

DRILL 4.4   Developing the Short Angle and Deep-Down-the-Line Volley

AIMS
To improve the execution of the short angle and deep-down-the-line volley; to develop a better tactical awareness of when to play each shot.

LEVEL
Intermediate to advanced

DESCRIPTION
The coach begins this sequence of drills by feeding a player two volleys. The player starts behind the service line and moves in as the coach begins to feed. The coach stands in the middle of the court, just inside the baseline. The player hits her first volley deep down the line, and then moves farther forward to hit her second volley as a short angle. She should alternate between the forehand and backhand side (i.e., she hits two forehand volleys, moves back to behind the service line, and moves in again to hit two backhand volleys). Short angle and deep line targets should be in place for her to aim for.

VARIATION
The player progresses to hitting a variety of feeds (i.e., balls hit with different height, spin, pace, and direction) while maintaining the same sequence of volley targets (i.e., deep line, then short angle). The coach should vary feeding positions as the player's competency increases. Finally, she is allowed to hit to any target at any time.

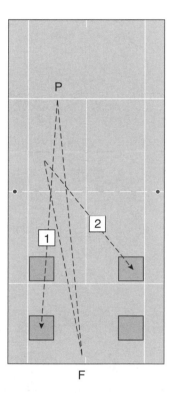

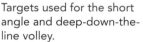

Targets used for the short angle and deep-down-the-line volley.

COACHING POINTS
The key to this drill lies in the shot selection of the player. She will likely want to hit a deep-down-the-line volley if she is behind the service line (because she is quite far from the net and the oncoming ball may be dropping low), compared to hitting a short angle volley when she is inside the service line (closer to her target and hitting the ball when it is at a higher point). This is why making the player hit to targets in this order, at the start of the drill, is important. The coach should also encourage a small split-step with balanced movement forward between each shot. When she is allowed to choose her volley target, her choice should depend on the difficulty of the feed (i.e., the tougher the feed, the more likely she should play the deep-down-the-line volley).

DRILL 4.5   Developing Power and Direction of the Smash

AIMS
To improve the power of a player's smash; to help her disguise its direction.

LEVEL
All

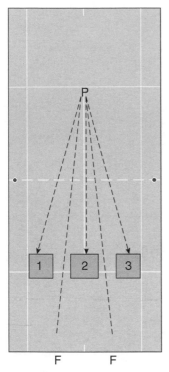

The three short T targets for the smash (1, 2, and 3).

DESCRIPTION
The coach starts by giving the player single-ball lobs from a corner position on the baseline. The player is positioned just inside the service line and is asked to hit the smash onto the opposite service line. The player must try to hit the smash with enough power so that the ball bounces above the shoulders of the coach on the baseline. As this shot develops, the coach begins to instruct the player where to hit the smash while the lob is in the air. Three targets are allowed: the left T, the middle T, and the right T. The player should be able to adjust the direction of her smash to any of these three short targets at the last moment.

VARIATION
The coach can experiment with how late he or she can give instruction before the player contacts the ball. The drill can progress to playing the point out after the lob feed (with a playing partner or coach still calling the smash direction). It's interesting to note how many points the player still wins—despite her opponent knowing where the smash is going!

COACHING POINTS
A loose wrist will give the player the chance to bounce the smash high enough. This can be a very difficult ball to defend against because the ball bounces with power *and* height at an opponent. Also, a loose wrist will give the player the chance to change the direction of the smash at the last moment, increasing its disguise in a similar way to how the direction of a serve can be disguised. The key to this drill, though, is the fact that the net player will still win many points, even though her opponent knows where the smash is going. If this is the case, it demonstrates that the power of the smash is more important than its accuracy.

DRILL 4.6   **Winning With the Smash**

AIMS
To improve shot selection of, positioning of, and confidence with the smash.

LEVEL
All

DESCRIPTION
The coach feeds a mixture of high balls from a variety of positions along the baseline. The player, who is positioned on the service line, must quickly perceive the flight path of the oncoming ball and decide whether to smash, drive volley, or volley it. The player shouts 'smash', 'drive', or 'volley' as soon as she makes her choice. She receives bonus points for a correct decision, even if she misses the shot. The drill progresses to playing the point out from the coach's feed.

VARIATION
The coach feeds an extremely high ball in the air that the player must allow to bounce. She must quickly decide whether to hit a bounce smash (i.e., smashing the ball after its bounce) or a shoulder-high groundstroke. She then plays the point out from this feed, and the coach notes whether she follows this shot in to the net.

COACHING POINTS
As well as using good perception and decision-making skills, the player must position herself correctly for each type of shot. She should be positioned underneath the ball for the smash (and bounce smash), compared to being positioned to the side of the ball for the volley (and drive volley). The coach should encourage quick movement to the front and back of the court, as well as across the court, and note how early the player makes her decision by considering the time that elapses between the feed and her shout.

DRILL 4.7   Combining the Volley and Smash

AIM
To improve volley and smash technique by hitting four-ball combinations.

LEVEL
All

DESCRIPTION
This drill requires the player to hit three alternate volleys before finishing the sequence with a smash. The player starts from behind the service line and moves closer to the net after each shot. Short angle and deep line targets are placed on the court for the player to aim at, and she is allowed to hit to any of these on any shot. She is asked to hit her smash into a more central area (around the middle of the court) because it is less important for this shot to be hit with accuracy. The coach mixes up the baseline position from where the balls are fed after every sequence to keep the drill realistic to a match situation. As the player becomes more proficient with her volley, she is asked to hit any combination of three volleys (including different height, spin, pace, and direction) instead of alternate ones. Finally, she is asked to hit any combination of four shots, including the smash, at any time during the sequence. Introducing the smash at any time will help the player develop her anticipation and perception skills because she will need to be able to read the flight path of the ball quickly to get into a good hitting position.

VARIATIONS
1. The coach feeds a sequence of high-low-high-low volleys. This is a very physical combination that demands strong use of the legs and good control of the racket face.

2. The coach varies the number of balls fed in one sequence and the ratio between volleys and lobs. The next feed is linked to the quality of the last shot played; that is, a very strong volley would merit an easier following feed (implying that the opponent has been put under pressure). Also, the coach encourages the player to leave any feeds that she thinks are going out. This helps to improve her perception and decision-making skills.

3. The player plays the point out after the lob feed. The drill moves quickly from a closed practice to an open one so the player must anticipate when the lob is going to be hit. The coach varies the difficulty of the lob so that the player plays the point out from different tactical situations also.

COACHING POINTS
The player should take a small split-step between each shot and move forward after each ball, even though she may be lobbed. As a rule, it is usually easier to move backward and *up* to a smash than it is to move forward and *down* to a volley. Many female players are guilty of hanging back too far from the net, allowing an opponent too much space to hit the passing shot into.

DRILL 4.8 Playing the Volley and Smash With Consistency

AIM
To improve the consistency of a player's volley and smash.

LEVEL
All

DESCRIPTION
The net player chooses an area to volley from at the net (i.e., left, middle, or right) and volleys back to her opponent, who is positioned in one half of the court on the baseline (i.e., either the deuce or advantage court). The baseline player is encouraged to hit aggressive groundstrokes at the net player, who can change her volley position at any time. The baseline player must hit to wherever the net player moves to. The drill remains closed until the baseline player chooses to hit the lob. When this happens, the point is played out in the full court. This means that the smash can be hit anywhere, and the baseline player tries to win the point with accurate passing shots or lobs. Play continues to seven points; points count only when the lob has been played.

VARIATIONS
1. Baseline players are allowed to hit only *topspin* lobs when choosing to lob. This encourages careful shot selection and a greater awareness of attacking opportunities.
2. The point starts only when the net player hits a drop volley or when the baseline player forces the net player into hitting a half volley. A half volley is a ball that is hit using volley technique but bounces just before contact; it is usually played against a ball hit very low to the net player's feet.
3. Players play the point out automatically after a certain number of volleys have been hit into the half court.

COACHING POINTS
The net player should change her volley position frequently throughout the rally. The coach should encourage early anticipation of the lob and/or chip down to the feet of the net player. The net player should start the rally from behind the service line and move forward after each shot. This movement is crucial to keeping the drill realistic because players should avoid practicing the volley from a static position. The coach should encourage a big target area for the smash, with balanced recovery and movement back in to the net.

DRILL 4.9   Using the Intercept Volley in Doubles

AIM
To develop the intercept volley in doubles by encouraging early anticipation, aggressive movement, and a relevant target to aim for.

LEVEL
All

DESCRIPTION
Two doubles teams (A and B) oppose each other by setting up in a one-up/one-back formation. Starting from a hand-feed, the two baseline players begin rallying crosscourt to each other (they are allowed to hit only crosscourt to begin with). The net player from team A is encouraged to intercept the oncoming groundstroke at any time by moving across the net in a diagonal, forward direction. Her aim should be to hit down to the feet of her opponent at the net or down the middle of the court if her opponent is standing too far wide. The net player from team B must try to defend against this intercept volley by using quick reactions and movement. The point is played out once the intercept volley has been used. After team A's net player has played five intercept volley points, the roles are switched to allow team B's net player the chance to intercept instead. Upon completion, each baseline player changes position with her net partner, and the drill is repeated. The drill progresses to allowing both net players the chance to intercept within the same rally. Finally, the baseline players are given the chance to lob or hit down the line if they see their opposing net player moving across to intercept too early.

COACHING POINTS
Players should use the intercept volley as much as possible. The net player should move forward to the ball (rather than just sideways), and she should choose the correct ball to intercept (i.e., is she under too much pressure or can she dominate?). The coach should note where she hits the volley to and how well the opposing team defends against it. Bonus points are given for calculated risk taking, and points are subtracted for missed opportunities.

DRILL 4.10 **Working as a Doubles Team at the Net**

AIMS
To improve teamwork, communication, and shot selection for a doubles team when both players are playing at the net.

LEVEL
All

DESCRIPTION
The coach is positioned on one side of the baseline (in a returning position) with both players at the net. The coach hits a series of single-ball feeds of varying difficulty that the pair must volley or smash against. The players are encouraged to play down the middle of the court when under pressure and wide of the court when able to dominate. They score a point for every correct decision made (even if they miss the shot). The coach judges their decisions first; then the pair judges its own shot selections (i.e., the player *not* hitting the ball judges her partner's choice of shot, and vice versa).

VARIATION
The drill progresses to playing the point out from the feed, and the pair plays back down the middle to the coach until they choose to hit the wide shot into the space that finishes the point. The coach and the players should discuss each player's shot selections relative to her tactical positions on the court.

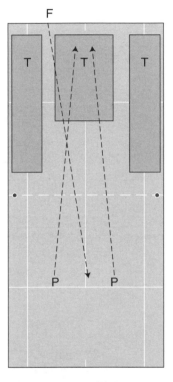

Using wide and middle targets when developing teamwork at the net.

COACHING POINTS
The coach should encourage clear communication and quick decision making within the pair by deliberately feeding balls down the middle of the court. The coach should try to tempt both players to go for the same ball. This will help them designate clear responsibilities at the net. Players should use 'parallel play' by moving forward, sideways, and backward together because they must not leave any big gaps on the court. The coach should note the target areas the pair uses for the majority of defensive volleys and smashes that they hit, compared to those they use when in more dominant positions.

DRILL 4.11 **Standing Ground When Under Pressure at the Net**

AIM
To help a player develop her quick reaction volley when under intense pressure at the net.

LEVEL
Intermediate to advanced

DESCRIPTION
The player positions herself between the service line and the net, and the coach faces her on the opposite service line. The coach feeds four volleys in quick succession, aiming at the body of the player while moving forward after each feed. The player must stand her ground and try to play as many of these quick-fire volleys back into the court as possible. This exercise helps the player develop greater control of her racket head while under intense time pressure. She faces 10 sets of four-ball combinations, and she scores a point for every volley she plays into the court.

VARIATION
The coach stands just inside the baseline and feeds the player a volley down the middle of the court. The point is played out down the middle only, and the coach tries to immediately pressure the net player by moving in to the net at any opportunity. The player tries to keep the coach at the back by volleying deep and tries to prevent being attacked if the coach approaches by keeping the ball low. The two can experiment by using different playing patterns (e.g., rally crosscourt to the forehand or backhand sides).

COACHING POINTS
The player should be encouraged to hold her position at the net rather than move backward to gain more time. She should play with a strong wrist and strong posture and with a contact point in front of her body (to allow her to use the pace of her opponent's shot most effectively). The coach should note whether she uses the forehand or backhand volley when the ball is hit hard and close to her body. Players commonly hit the backhand volley from this position because it is easier to play the ball in front of the body (i.e., the elbow doesn't cramp the body as much as it does on the forehand side). Also, the player should make space for herself by swerving her upper body away from the ball if she doesn't have time to move her feet.

DRILL 4.12 **Defending the Net as a Doubles Team**

AIM
To improve a doubles pair's ability to defend the net with strong reflex volleys and good teamwork when under pressure.

LEVEL
All

DESCRIPTION
Four players are on court with one pair positioned at the net and one pair positioned on the baseline. The drill begins with two separate rallies: each net player volleying crosscourt to her baseline opponent. As soon as one of the rallies breaks down, the other rally immediately becomes an open doubles point with all four players involved. The objective for the baseline pair is to move in to the net together by forcing their opponents back. The pair at the net must try to hold their positions no matter how much pressure they face.

VARIATION
The drill is the same, starting with two separate rallies, but all four players are positioned at the net. This means that both pairs hit volley-to-volley rallies, and the point is played out after one of the rallies finishes. The players can experiment by starting the drill with two rallies played down the line rather than crosscourt.

COACHING POINTS
This drill greatly improves players' perception and reaction skills. All volleys should be hit with a contact point in front of the body and a short 'punch' or 'block' instead of a swing. Every net player should use a small split-step, even when she has very little time between her volleys. Again, quick and clear communication between partners is vital. The coach should note how each pair moves at the net: Do they move together as one unit, or do they separate when under pressure?

DRILL 4.13 **Developing Tactical and Technical Anticipation**

AIMS
To develop a player's tactical and technical anticipation; to improve the efficiency of her movement when playing at the net.

LEVEL
All

DESCRIPTION
The player is positioned between the service line and the baseline, and the coach (or practice partner) stands on the middle of the opposite baseline. The coach feeds a short ball for the player to hit and approach the net with. The player can approach to either side of the coach, who replies by playing a passing shot or lob. At any time, the coach can stop the ball just before hitting it and ask the net player where she thinks the ball is going. She scores a point for every correct answer. The coach should stop the rally after he or she has played the passing shot or lob to study the position and movement of the net player.

VARIATION
Players play the point out and receive bonus points for early anticipation of the coach's passing shots and lobs.

COACHING POINTS
The player should follow the direction of her approach in to the net (as opposed to simply moving to the middle of the court) because this will allow her to cover the most appropriate area at the net. The coach should encourage a small split-step after moving forward between shots. The coach should note whether the player is able to read the tactical position of her opponent, and whether she notices any differences in stroke technique as a result.

Opposing the Net Player

The final tactical situation in women's tennis occurs when an opponent approaches and plays at the net. As mentioned earlier, female players are finding different ways of playing from the net, and it is important for the baseline player to be ready for every form of attack. In general, most players enjoy having an opponent at the net to aim past and are comfortable moving across the baseline to hit a passing shot or lob. However, the baseline player can experience real difficulties if her opponent approaches behind a very strong shot (hit with pace *and* width) or a short, low ball that forces the player to quickly move forward to meet it. Approaching when a player least expects it (i.e., as a surprise tactic) can also catch her off guard. Therefore, being aware of an opponent's movement and court position is vital, as is an ability to move quickly and efficiently into short and wide positions. This chapter will study these important issues in singles and doubles play, along with how to help a player make the right choice of shot, depending on her tactical position in each point.

Two-Ball Pass

I loved having a target to aim for at the net and would try to make my opponent play as many first volleys as possible.

—Elena Tatarkova, Former Top 50 Singles and Top 10 Doubles Player on the WTA Tour

Many players believe that they must hit a winning passing shot or lob as soon as their opponent approaches the net. This is simply not the case, particularly in the early stages of a match when it is important to test the volleying ability of an opponent. Indeed, many players who lack confidence at the net will try too hard with their volley, making an unforced error in the process. In some cases, the opponent may not actually want to be at the net; she is only there because she has been brought in by a very short ball! It is important, therefore, to make the opponent play the volley and smash to assess her competency. Knowing that an opponent lacks confidence at the net will take pressure off a player's passing shot and lob.

To test an opponent, many experienced players use the two-ball pass tactic to great effect. This tactic requires a player to hit a high-percentage passing shot (usually crosscourt or down the middle of the court) with the aim of making an opponent play a volley. Very often, the opponent doesn't hit this volley well, giving the player a chance to play a simple second passing shot or lob. This is usually more effective than trying to win the point immediately with the first passing shot or lob, which can often be a more difficult shot. Sometimes the opponent at the net is put off balance or placed in a difficult position after the first testing passing

Hitting a high-percentage passing shot when on the run will often prove effective.

shot. This often opens up a more obvious space past her for the second passing shot to be played into. The two-ball pass tactic applies, in particular, against an opponent who does not usually approach the net because she lacks confidence in her volley and smash. There is less chance that this player will volley well enough, making it even more important for the baseline player to make her play!

To practice the two-ball pass tactic, see drill 5.1 on page 170.

Lob

As discussed in chapter 4, the smash is a shot that many female players do not execute well—particularly those who rarely play at the net (these are often the players who serve poorly also, because the two techniques are very similar). As a result, the lob can be used as a strong weapon in the women's game.

The lob is hit high over the head of the net player either with topspin or as a blocked slice. The topspin lob requires fast racket head speed that brushes up the back of the ball (similar to groundstroke and drive volley technique). This spin allows a player to hit the ball high and fast through the air, knowing that the spin will drop the ball down quickly into the court. The blocked lob is often used when a player needs more control of the oncoming ball. This shot is hit as a blocking action rather than swinging action (similar to volley technique), giving a player easier control of her racket head. Such contrasting techniques mean that these two shots are usually played in different tactical situations. The blocked lob is frequently used when a baseline player is under pressure—either from the pace of the oncoming ball or her position on the court—whereas the topspin lob is used more when she is in an attacking position.

Using the lob *early* in a match can be a good investment because it shows the opponent that the baseline player possesses more than one passing shot option. Even if she loses the point, she will force her opponent to cover this potential shot next time with the possibility of her hanging back slightly when approaching. This can create more space around the net to hit the passing shot into.

Experienced players will hit the lob more often as a second shot in a two-ball sequence. This is because an opponent is usually positioned closer to the net after hitting her first volley, creating more space behind her for the lob to be hit into. This shot is used to great effect when an opponent has been brought in with a drop shot, or when she has had to play a short, low volley down at her feet.

The direction of the lob must be carefully considered in the context of today's game. In the past, players have been taught to lob over the backhand side of their opponent, because the high backhand volley is very difficult to execute. Most players today, however, move efficiently around their backhand side to hit the inside-out forehand groundstroke, a similar movement pattern to hitting the smash from the backhand side. Also, players are now comfortable hitting the high backhand drive volley from this position. Therefore, it is worth considering hitting the lob over the *forehand* side instead, because this shot is rarely practiced and can be very awkward for the opponent to hit if out of position.

🎾 Coaching Tip

Players will improve their movement to the passing shot and lob by practicing as many different movement patterns as possible.

Efficient movement to play the passing shot or lob will be rewarded through an increase in the pace of the shot, more accuracy, and greater time pressure applied to an opponent at the net. This applies equally to a deep ball (requiring movement across the baseline into a space or behind the baseline out of a space) or a short ball (requiring movement up the court). Naturally, the better the player's court position is, the more shot options that are available to her, which helps prevent her opponent from being able to tactically anticipate as effectively.

As mentioned in chapter 4, the short angle volley can cause the baseline player the most trouble because it requires her to move diagonally to the ball. This movement pattern should, therefore, be taught from an early age and be incorporated into a player's technique when playing from the baseline. This is an important point because it is very difficult to develop technique without incorporating movement. Perception, reaction, and movement all strongly influence how the ball is actually hit.

To practice the tactics discussed in this section, see drills 5.2 and 5.3 on pages 171 and 172.

Defending With the Double Bluff

When our opponents are at the net applying pressure, we try to hit through the middle of the court at all times. Occasionally we might try to lob or hit the low rolling angle. Obviously we will try to come in if we get the opportunity.

—Cara Black, Two-Time Wimbledon Doubles Champion (2004 and 2005)

Having to defend the smash or volley when under pressure can be very challenging, yet a lot of fun, for the player on the baseline. Despite usually being the underdog to win the point, she can still have a strong influence over the outcome of the point by using the double bluff tactic. This requires a player to *fake* a movement across the baseline (as if to defend the other side of the court) before returning to her original position as the opponent is about to hit her shot. To her opponent's surprise, the ball is often hit in the direction of the player instead of into the space! This sudden change of movement can also be enough to distract her opponent from executing a good shot. The double bluff is often used by the baseline player who is the underdog to win the point. In other words, the net player is in a strong position to dictate with her smash, and the baseline player is in a more defensive position.

In figure 5.1 the baseline player has hit a lob (1) over the backhand side of her right-handed opponent at the net. She fakes a movement across the court as if to defend the deuce court, before returning to the advantage court as her opponent is about to smash (2). To the opponent's surprise, the baseline player is in position to hit a passing shot crosscourt or down the line (3).

To practice the double bluff tactic, see drill 5.4 on page 173.

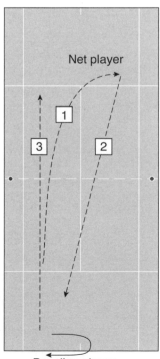

FIGURE 5.1 Defending the smash by using the double bluff tactic.

Shot selection in doubles is crucial when both opponents are at the net. Much depends on the amount of pressure the baseline player is under (presuming that her partner is at the net also) because this will directly affect where she hits the ball. As a rule, the baseline player is advised not to hit down the same side of the court (i.e., down the line) when under pressure because this will give an opponent the chance to hit an aggressive angle back. Instead, she has three main options (see figure 5.2): hitting down the middle between the two net players (1), hitting crosscourt (2), or lobbing crosscourt (3). All of these shots carry a higher margin of error and aim to neutralise an opposing team's advantage. Note how her partner is prepared to adjust her net position based on how much pressure they are being put under as a team. She may choose to move backward to defend more effectively in this situation.

The reverse is true when the baseline player is in a more dominant position. In this situation, she is encouraged to hit aggressively down the middle or down the line against her opponents at the net. These two shots will potentially create more space on the court for her to hit her next shot into, or for her partner to volley into. The middle ball will pull the players together, whereas the down-the-line ball will push them apart. In figure 5.3 the baseline player, again positioned

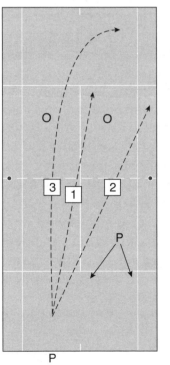

FIGURE 5.2 Options for the baseline player when under pressure by an opposing team at the net.

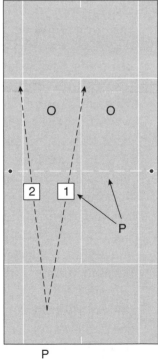

FIGURE 5.3 Options for the baseline player when in a dominant position against an opposing team at the net.

in the advantage court, holds a more dominant position over her opponents. Her two best options are to hit down the middle (1) or down the line (2). In this situation, her partner will be looking to move forward to intercept with an aggressive volley, depending on the amount of pressure her opponents are under. Note also how the lob is often used more from a defensive position than from an attacking one. This is because a high, defensive lob gives the team valuable time to reorganise themselves into a better court position. This contrasts with an attacking position in which their aim is to take time away from their opponents by hitting through them. (The same principles apply from the deuce court as from the advantage court.)

To practice the tactics discussed in this section, see drill 5.5 on page 174.

Assessing Net Play

Measuring the effectiveness of a player at the net, or when her opponent plays at the net, is done in the same way as measuring the serve, return, and baseline play. This information enables the player and coach to assess the effectiveness of the player's net play, as well as her passing shot and lob, allowing for more effective practice of these shots in the future. For example, it can show whether a player is more effective using the instinctive or planned approach, which volley she is strongest playing, how often she wins the point with her smash, and whether she has more success hitting her passing shot crosscourt or down the line. Also, having a record of how and when an opponent approaches the net will help when playing the same player in the future. Understanding an opponent's favourite net play patterns will help a player make a specific tactical plan. For example, if an opponent is shown to be ineffective at the net, the player may plan to bring her in even more next time.

The most common three tools used for measuring net play are a match flow chart, a court diagram, and calculating net play percentages. Figure 5.4 is a net play summary. To calculate the various percentages, divide the first number in the sequence by the second number and multiply by 100.

Net Play Summary

_____ (number of first volleys hit in) / _____ (number of first volley attempts)

= _____ percentage of first volleys made

_____ (number of points won at the net) / _____ (total number of net play points won)

= _____ percentage of net play points won

_____ (number of points won using the sneak) / _____ (total number of sneaks attempted)

= _____ percentage of sneak attempts that were successful

_____ (number of unreturnable smashes hit) / _____ (total number of smashes attempted)

= _____ percentage of unreturnable smashes

_____ (number of points won using the two-ball pass) / _____ (total number of two-ball pass attempts)

= _____ percentage of two-ball pass attempts that were successful

_____ (number of points won using the lob) / _____ (total number of lob attempts)

= _____ percentage of lob attempts that were successful

FIGURE 5.4   **Net play summary.**

Summary

☐ Many experienced players use the two-ball pass tactic when an opponent approaches the net. This requires a player to make her opponent play her first volley by hitting a high-percentage passing shot (either crosscourt or down the middle of the court) before trying to hit a winning pass or lob with her second shot. This tactic applies, in particular, against an opponent who is not confident playing from the net.

☐ The lob is used as a weapon more often in women's tennis than it is in the men's game. Using it early in a match can pay dividends because it forces an opponent to cover an extra passing shot option for the rest of the match. Hitting the lob as a second shot in a two-ball pass sequence is also popular because there is more space behind the net player for it to be hit into after the first volley has been played (because the net player should be moving forward). It is worth considering playing the lob over the forehand side also, given that most players now comfortably move around their backhand side.

☐ A player must move efficiently before playing the passing shot or lob. This involves moving across or up the court into a space, as well as moving behind the baseline out of a space. Players need to practice moving to the short angle volley, in particular, because it requires them to move diagonally to the ball.

☐ A player should experiment by using the double bluff tactic when defending from the baseline. This requires her to fake a movement across the court before returning to her original side. This often results in her opponent hitting the ball to her without meaning to.

☐ In doubles, the baseline player should hit across the court (i.e., crosscourt, down the middle between the players at the net, or lob crosscourt) when she is under pressure and both opponents are at the net. In a more dominant position, she can afford to hit more aggressively down the line, or through the middle of the court.

DRILL 5.1   **Using the Two-Ball Pass Tactic**

AIM
To develop the use of the two-ball pass tactic, including good shot selection and movement to every ball.

LEVEL
All

DESCRIPTION
The baseline player feeds a short ball for the coach (or practice partner) to approach with. The coach approaches the net with this ball into a predetermined area of the court. The baseline player must hit her first pass down the middle of the court, straight at the coach (who plays this volley anywhere), before trying to win the point with her second shot as a pass or lob. The player should find that there is more space to hit into—past the coach—on her second shot than on her first. The drill should start with the baseline player knowing where the approach shot will be hit (i.e., to her forehand or backhand side), before progressing to a more open situation.

VARIATIONS
1. The player hits her first pass down to the feet of the net player (using either slice or heavy topspin). This shot forces the opponent to hit a more defensive volley (or half volley) up over the net, allowing the player to dominate with her next shot.

2. If the player chooses to hit a lob as a second shot, she must hit it with aggressive topspin.

COACHING POINTS
The coach should keep track of how many points the baseline player wins by playing the two-ball pass tactic. The coach should also encourage good shot selection; that is, note where the player hits her second pass (crosscourt or down the line) or whether she chooses to lob instead. These choices will depend on the net position of the opponent. Also, the coach should encourage quick recovery between shots with balanced movement straight to each ball.

DRILL 5.2　**Using the Aggressive and Defensive Lob**

AIM
To improve the quality and shot selection of the lob.

LEVEL
All

DESCRIPTION
The coach (or practice partner) is positioned just inside the service line, and the player is positioned in the middle of the baseline. The player hand-feeds a low volley to the coach, who replies with a deep volley anywhere. The player must play a lob as a second shot, and the coach hits the smash back to a predetermined area. The point is played out after this pattern is completed. The players play first to seven points before switching roles.

VARIATIONS
1. Three players are on court, one net player and two baseline players. The net player can volley and smash anywhere, earning two points for a winning smash (because there is less space to hit into).

2. The pattern can be reversed by feeding a lob first followed by a low volley and then another lob. This encourages the baseline player to push and pull the net player from the back to the front of the court. The net player should start the drill by positioning herself inside the service line (or even by touching the net with her racket).

3. The baseline player(s) can only use the lob. This means that a variety of lobs will be hit—both aggressive and defensive ones.

4. This is an excellent drill to use with four players on the court also. One pair plays from the net and the other pair plays from the baseline. The players on the baseline must lob twice before playing the point out. Again, winning smashes are worth two points.

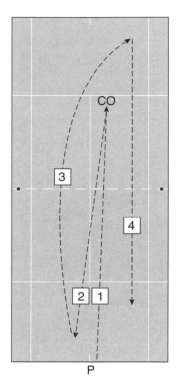

The player feeds a low volley (1) to the coach (or practice partner), who replies with a deep volley to the baseline (2). The player then lobs crosscourt, over the right-hander's backhand side (3). The coach hits the smash into the deuce court (4), and the point is played out.

COACHING POINTS
Players should hit the first lob aggressively with topspin, over either the forehand or backhand side. The coach should point out that a player hitting the lob crosscourt has more court space to hit into, compared to the player hitting the lob down the line. This is because the court is longer crosscourt than down the line. When the baseline player chooses to lob her opponent, the coach should note whether there is enough space behind her to lob into.

DRILL 5.3   Improving the Running Passing Shot and Lob

AIMS
To improve a player's ability to hit the passing shot down the line and the lob crosscourt while on the run; to develop the ability to quickly read the flight path of the oncoming ball and the position of the net player.

LEVEL
Intermediate to advanced

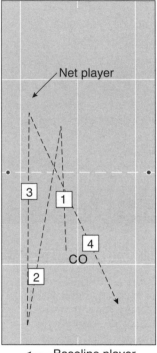

The four-ball pattern of play for the running passing shot drill.

DESCRIPTION
The coach stands on the middle T and feeds either a forehand or backhand volley to the net player, who volleys down the line. The baseline player moves across the court (and up the court if necessary) to hit a running passing shot back down the line. The net player then tries to hit a short angle volley with this ball. The drill stops after this four-ball pattern and is then repeated.

VARIATION
Once this pattern is established, the baseline player introduces the crosscourt lob as an alternative. The net player hits the smash, but only down the line (away from the coach in the middle of the court). This drill is good to use with three players on court—one player at the net and two players taking turns hitting the running passing shot or lob.

COACHING POINTS
The baseline player should make her opponent play as many volleys as possible. She should hit around the outside edge of the ball to bring it back into the court (note the direction of the passing shot in the figure). The baseline player should hit the lob when the net player is particularly close to the net. She must be able to recognise her opponent's net position clearly to be able to do this. Also, the baseline player should read the direction of the volley as soon as possible, because this will help her get into position in enough time.

DRILL 5.4   Defending With the Double Bluff

AIM
To improve a player's ability to defend by using the double bluff tactic when lobbing.

LEVEL
Intermediate to advanced

DESCRIPTION
The player is positioned on the middle of the baseline with the coach (or practice partner) positioned at the net. The player feeds an easy ball down the middle for the coach to volley into the corner with (the player and coach have agreed on the corner beforehand). The point is played out from here, and the player is allowed to use only the lob throughout the rally. The baseline player wins two points to the net player's one when she successfully uses the double bluff tactic.

VARIATIONS
1. The player can use one passing shot in the rally (the rest of her shots can only be lobs).
2. The player's first shot after the feed must be a lob; then she can use any shot to win the point with.

COACHING POINTS
The coach can highlight the use of the double bluff by asking the player to start to move across the baseline earlier than normal (i.e., as soon as she hits her lob). She can choose whether to return to her original position or to continue across the baseline to cover the other side. She should use both movements to create variety and uncertainty for her opponent. Also, the coach should highlight the importance of lobbing deep over an opponent—even if this means making an error. This is generally a better option than giving an opponent the chance to hit a confidence-boosting winner against a shorter lob.

DRILL 5.5 Playing Against a Doubles Team at the Net

AIM
To improve a player's shot selection when playing against a doubles team at the net.

LEVEL
All

DESCRIPTION
Four players are on court; one pair is positioned at the net, while the other pair is positioned in a one-up/one-back formation. The coach stands behind the baseline player and feeds a ball for the net players to volley (back to the baseline player). The coach's feeds vary in difficulty throughout the drill. The point is played out from here; the shot selection of the baseline player depends on the amount of pressure she is under. Players play to seven points before rotating positions on the court so that every player has a chance to play from the baseline position.

VARIATION
The coach feeds a lob to the pair at the net and notes how the baseline player's partner adjusts her net position, depending on the quality of the lob.

COACHING POINTS
The coach should encourage the baseline player to attack down the middle or line when in control of the point, as opposed to defending down the middle or crosscourt when under pressure. How quickly does she read each tactical position, and how appropriately does her partner react at the net? The coach should encourage clear communication between the partners, especially when the lob is hit (because this shot gives them more time to organise themselves).

Developing a Game Style

A game style defines how a player plays the game. It is shaped by her physical and technical ability, as well as her personality, and is built through relevant practice and competitive match play experience. Unlike a tactic or a pattern of play, it is not something that can be changed or adjusted momentarily. A player's game style represents everything about her. It's what she *is* on the tennis court.

When we remember the great female players of the past such as King, Navratilova, Evert, Graf, and Seles, we immediately think of *how* they played the game. We think of their mental toughness, their athletic ability, the great shots they played, and the tactics they used. All of these factors helped shape their own unique game style—the picture we now remember them by. Indeed, today's top players will also be recognised immediately by their game styles. A definite style of play allows a player to develop tactics and patterns that suit her best. It allows her to set specific goals in practice and helps to sharpen her focus in matches because she plays with a stronger sense of purpose. This, in turn, enhances her level of confidence and promotes a greater feeling of control over her ultimate tennis journey.

This chapter starts by analysing the four key stages of tactical development that a player will experience throughout her tennis journey—from beginner to pro level. It will then study how a player goes about developing her own game style by helping her identify her strengths and build them into winning patterns of play. It will discuss the importance of good decision making and problem solving, and of taking responsibility, and how these personal factors influence the direction of a player's game style.

Stages of Tactical Development

It takes 10 years and 10,000 hours of practice, training, and competition to develop an expert in anything—and that includes tennis.
—Anne Pankhurst, USTA Coaching Education Department

The tactical development of a tennis player takes many years to evolve. As a player progresses, her technical, physical, and mental skills evolve with her, and these skills directly influence how she plays the game of tennis. As a result, her game as a beginner will differ greatly from her game as a pro. For this reason she must build a strong and varied foundation of skills that will allow her to develop her own game style in the future. Four key stages in a female player's tennis development are widely recognised. Junior stages are based on chronological age;

senior stages are based on tennis playing experience. Junior guidelines are based on the Lawn Tennis Association's Long-Term Player Development model.

Stage 1: Junior: 5–9 years old   Senior: Beginner level
Stage 2: Junior: 9–12 years old   Senior: Improver level
Stage 3: Junior: 12–16 years old   Senior: Club/regional level
Stage 4: Junior: 16 years old +   Senior: National/international level

Junior player stages differ between girls and boys because girls tend to mature earlier than boys do, both physically and mentally, which allows them to develop their game style at a younger age. In fact, it is often argued that women's tennis is an early specialisation sport because of this, whereas men's tennis is a medium to late specialisation sport. This means that the windows of opportunity to develop female players open and close earlier than they do for male players. Recognising this, and knowing what to practice within each stage, is crucial. The rate at which an adult beginner progresses through these stages will depend very much on the amount of tennis she plays, the coaching she receives, and her previous sporting experiences (people with strong sporting backgrounds can often develop their tennis skills quickly because there is a certain amount of crossover from other sports). The four stages of tactical development are studied in more detail in the following sections.

Stage 1

The priority for a beginner is to develop techniques that allow her to play the game with consistency and variety. Minimising technical weaknesses is crucial during stage 1 and stage 2 because weaknesses will only hinder a player's tactical development as she progresses. She will not be ready to develop a specific game style at this stage, but instead, will be looking to build a wide variety of skills that will help her do this in the future. This is a key point. At stage 1 the main emphasis is on developing a player's coordination, movement, and reception skills, as well as making tennis fun. Usually, she will have little tennis experience, and she will find it difficult to judge the height and depth of the oncoming ball. Her reaction speed will be relatively slow and her movement not particularly quick to and around the ball.

During stage 1 a player generally plays only in the first three game situations: serving, returning, and playing from the baseline against her opponent. (She may have to hit some volleys, but this will usually be because she is out of position rather than because she is choosing to approach the net.) At this stage her three main tactics within all three game situations will be simple: get the ball over the net and in the court, move her opponent around the court, and recover to a good baseline position between shots.

For the young player (5 to 9 years old), many coaches believe in smaller courts and softer balls. These give her more time to receive the oncoming ball and greater control over her shots, allowing her to play the game more often! This is an important point because her tactical development will be greatly enhanced if she can experience a variety of playing situations rather than just learn how to hit the ball over the net.

Whether a beginner should learn technique or tactics first at this stage is an interesting debate. In the past, coaches would usually teach technique first. Players learned *how* to hit the ball before ever learning *where* to hit the ball. However, players would often find it difficult to apply these technical skills outside of their coaching lessons. As a result, coaches are now using a more games-based approach to teaching tennis, which is proving far more effective. Games-based coaching puts players in playing situations in which tactics and problem solving are encouraged, and in which specific tasks have to be fulfilled to play successfully. Improving technique is presented as a means of fulfilling these tasks; they learn what to do while learning how to do it.

Toward the end of this first stage, players should begin to realise that taking the ball out of the air is a tactical option. Therefore, they will experience some net play situations. Some players will deliberately approach the net at this stage, but usually only on very short balls. The lob will be hit more often than the passing shot because of the limited technical competence of both the net player and the baseline player. This applies in doubles play also, with the groundstroke and lob remaining the two most dominant shots at this stage.

As a player's technical and physical abilities develop, her preparation, movement, and balance will improve also, allowing for greater tactical variation at the completion of this stage. For a junior player, this means that she is able to play properly in the full court at around the age of 9. For an adult, this means being able to maintain a rally from a serving or returning situation on a regular basis. A player's understanding of the game, the rules, and the meaning of competition will also be developing alongside her tactical skills. As a result, both the junior and senior player will be able to play some kind of competitive match by the end of this stage, representing a significant milestone in her playing career.

The following is a summary of the tactical skills a player should be mastering as she reaches the end of stage 1:

When Serving

Gets the ball over the net and in the court

Places the serve in different parts of the service box

Places the serve deep in the service box

When Returning

Reads the direction of the serve quickly

Adjusts her returning position

Hits the return deep

Changes the flight path of the ball (higher, lower, and more angle)

Recovers quickly for her next shot

When Playing From the Baseline

Hits with height and depth

Moves to the wide ball quickly

Varies the flight path of her groundstroke

Stage 2

Stage 2 represents a crucial period in a player's development. It is during this stage that her own style of play is first introduced. From a tactical viewpoint, she will look to build her points in a more structured way (rather than simply react to each ball separately). Coordination, balance, and movement will continue to develop, enabling her to identify her specific strengths. A strong emphasis is placed on improving technique because this is recognised as the 'golden age' of learning for a player between 9 and 12 years old. In other words, a player in this stage is very receptive to new ideas and will quickly adapt to new tactics and techniques. As a result, a player will be expected to start playing in all five game situations (with more deliberate net play used especially) and will be practicing a wider range of shots as she begins to understand how she wants to play.

The adult player will also be able to focus more sharply on tactics and match play as the execution of her shots becomes more familiar (i.e., she will be moving from a cognitive to an associative stage of technical learning). This means that she will be able to use a sequence of shots to win the point with and will be able to think ahead because she has more of an understanding of the game and a wider choice of shots. At this level she will begin to play individual tournaments, which will prepare her to play team matches at club level in stage 3.

The following is a summary of the tactical skills a player should be mastering as she reaches the end of stage 2:

When Serving
Hits a variety of serves (with good placement and pace, but not necessarily spin)
Starts to recognise the first serve as an opportunity to attack

When Returning
Hits a variety of returns
Is able to neutralise a first serve by returning high and deep
Is able to attack a weak serve and maintain control of the rally

When Playing From the Baseline
Uses the short angle as a tactic
Surprises the opponent with variety (e.g., slice, drop shot, etc.)
Defends with height and depth
Wins with consistency

When Approaching and Playing at the Net
Uses the drive volley
Approaches on a midcourt ball
Finishes points with volleys and smashes
Starts playing as a team at the net in doubles

When an Opponent is at the Net
Plays the passing shot or lob
Uses the two-ball pass tactic
Plays with spin to the feet of the net player
Tries to take the net away from an opposing pair, in doubles, by hitting the lob

Stage 3

Presuming that a strong tactical and technical base has been built in stage 2, stage 3 presents a player with the opportunity to develop a very specific game style. Developing her strengths and combining them into recognisable patterns of play will therefore be the major tactical focus during this time. This stage is particularly important for a girl (12 to 16 years old) because she tends to mature earlier than her male counterpart. Her physical and mental capacities increase significantly during this time, allowing her to hit the ball with more pace, control, and spin. She is also able to bring a sharper, more mature focus to the court. Her ability to compete with senior players will help also because she will have more playing experiences and develop a wider knowledge base. (It is not uncommon to see players in this age group competing at the WTA Tour level.) Her personality is developing rapidly also, and this too will influence the way she plays. For example, a player who likes to take risks will play differently from a player who values safety and consistency. Also, players will have different levels of aggression, determination, and creativity—all of which will strongly influence their game styles.

The adult player will have had enough tennis experience in this stage to know how she plays best. Her practices will be geared around developing her strongest shots and linking them together into winning patterns of play. She will also be learning how to avoid exposing any potential weaknesses. Again, her game style will be taking a more recognisable shape as her shots and movement patterns become more natural (moving from an associative to an autonomous stage of learning). As a result, she will be expected to play competently in all five game situations (singles and doubles) by the end of this stage. She will be very experienced playing at club level at the end of this stage and may be ready to compete beyond her local county or district level.

The following is a summary of the tactical skills a player should be mastering as she reaches the end of stage 3:

When Serving

Increases the variety of direction, pace, and possibly spin (slice especially)

Starts to use the serve as the first shot in an attacking pattern of play (e.g., serve and groundstroke attack)

Takes an aggressive court position (inside the baseline) after the first serve has been hit

When Returning

Is able to change the flight path of the ball

Is able to change the direction of the ball

Neutralises effectively against a strong first serve

Returns from inside the baseline against most second serves

Develops patterns of play that start with an aggressive return (e.g., return and baseline control)

When Playing From the Baseline
   Plays with a definite game style
   Is able to build, attack, and defend from the baseline
   Plays with consistency, accuracy, and some variety
   Plays the shoulder-high attack
   Uses the high and low recovery shot
   Develops alternative strategies to counter difficult opponents

When Approaching and Playing at the Net
   Makes correct decisions regarding when to approach the net
   Uses the sneak approach and volley
   Plays with more anticipation at the net
   Uses the intercept volley in doubles

When an Opponent is at the Net
   Uses the lob more aggressively (topspin rather than slice)
   Continues using the two-ball pass
   Moves faster and hits with more strength when on the run
   Takes the net away from an opposing pair in doubles

Stage 4

In stage 4 a player should have a well-defined game style and should continually gain match experience through playing a variety of tournaments (preferably at home and abroad). She is learning to make quicker decisions and is problem-solving against opponents with different playing styles. She is able to switch between attacking and defensive tactics more easily and is comfortable playing her game on a variety of surfaces. She looks to maximise her strengths and minimise her weaknesses at every opportunity.

At the same time, a player will be learning to take more responsibility for her game, both on and off the court. A greater emphasis is placed on her mental skills because her core technical and physical skills have already been developed. For example, she will make decisions about how, where, when, and with whom to play and will learn to compete without always having the support of family, friends, and coaches. In other words, she will take *ownership* of her game. Decision making, problem solving, and player responsibility are all discussed in detail later in this chapter.

The following is a summary of the tactical skills a player should be mastering as she competes during stage 4:

When Serving

Plays with a variety of directions and paces on the first serve

Plays with a definite serving pattern from both sides that includes a favoured second shot

Uses the sneak volley, drive volley, and serve and volley tactic when appropriate

Uses a second serve that remains difficult to attack—by hitting with slice (and possibly topspin), accuracy, and variety of direction

When Returning

Neutralises a strong first serve by hitting crosscourt, inside-out, inside-in, or down the middle

Uses the blocked return as a deliberate tactic to slow the pace of the ball

Dominates an opponent by using specific second serve return tactics (e.g., return and groundstroke attack)

Approaches the net with a return, either instinctually or planned

When Playing From the Baseline

Plays with a definite game style

Builds a winning position consistently by using at least one favoured pattern of play

Uses variety for specific tactical situations

Plays the shoulder-high attack

Uses the high and low recovery shot

Develops alternative strategies to counter difficult opponents

When Approaching and Playing at the Net

Uses the sneak approach and planned approach to the net

Plays with a strong, reliable drive volley and smash

Uses the short angle volley when necessary

Uses a variety of set plays in doubles

When an Opponent is at the Net

Uses the topspin and blocked lob appropriately

Continues using the two-ball pass

Hits on the run effectively against a net target

Is able to chip low to the feet of the net player in singles and doubles

Chooses where to hit to a doubles team, depending on the pressure being faced

Developing Winning Patterns of Play

Winning patterns of play are the shot sequences players use to execute their most favoured tactics. They represent how they play best. For example, when playing the serve and groundstroke attack tactic from the deuce court, a player may regularly use a pattern of serving out wide and hitting an aggressive backhand into the space. These patterns form a crucial part of a player's overall game style because they signify how she wins the majority of her points. They will become recognisable during stage 3 of a player's tactical development and will be continually fine-tuned throughout stage 4. A player develops a winning pattern of play by simply combining her best shots as often as possible. Because most players are learning to dictate the point at the earliest opportunity, the modern game now requires at least one of these successful shots to be a serve or a return.

The key to developing a winning pattern of play is to understand where to hit the ball so that each shot builds on the previous one. For example, a right-handed player who loves to hit her forehand crosscourt will deliberately serve out wide from the advantage court in anticipation of receiving a 'late' return, hit down the line to her forehand side. Similarly, a player whose strength is playing at the net will work hard on the shots that get her there the most. In her case, this means developing a strong serve or return (or both), a variety of approach shots, and the ability to use the sneak tactic.

An effective way to develop winning patterns of play is by working on the *last* shot of the rally first, before moving backward to the start of the point. A player should consider her favourite attacking shot or position and then look at which shot sets up this situation best. She should repeat the process for each previous shot, back to the start of the point.

While developing winning patterns of play, a player must also develop patterns of play that minimise the exposure of her weaknesses to her opponent(s). She must try to prevent her opponent from exploiting any potential weakness by diverting play away from this area. For example, a player who has a much stronger forehand groundstroke than backhand doesn't want to get forced into playing long rallies from the baseline on the backhand side. Therefore, she develops her backhand down the line to force her opponent to hit to her forehand side more often. This will happen because most opponents will hit back crosscourt in response to a shot hit down their line. She will use this pattern as early as possible in the rally. In the same way, a player who has a weak second serve will minimise its exposure by developing a first serve technique that is very reliable. She will aim for a high first serve percentage throughout a match and will try to take the pressure off her service games by developing a strong returning game also.

Most winning patterns of play are first established at junior level, or club level for an adult (during stage 3 in particular), and are simply improved on as a player reaches higher playing levels. To develop such patterns, a player must first become aware of where her strengths lie. Younger players, in particular, often play matches without any real purpose because they don't yet know what they are good at. They simply react to their opponent's game without having their own plan in place. Once they have a clear idea as to what their best shots are, they can start combining them into more decisive patterns of play.

The Tactical Profile Form in figure 6.1 will encourage a player to reflect on her performances. It will help her to understand how she likes to play and help her, and her coach, build her strengths into winning patterns of play. Figure 6.2 shows a completed example. The hypothetical player in this example has a clear picture of how she wants to play the game because she is very aware of her strengths. As a result, she is able to highlight specific drills and practices that will help combine these strengths into definite patterns of play. She also understands the relevant technical, physical, and mental skills that she needs to make this happen. She has a great chance of achieving her competition goals because all aspects of her game are working together to achieve her outcome.

Personal Factors

I like to win by myself, and if I lose I like to take responsibility that I'm the one that lost.

—Tatiana Golovin

The tactical decisions that a player makes, and the amount of responsibility she takes for these decisions, will significantly influence her success on the match court by the time she reaches stage 4 of her tennis development. She will constantly be asked to problem-solve as she pits

Figure 6.1 Sample tactical profile form.

Name: Date:	Player's Signature: Coach's Signature:
My game style	
Role model(s)	
Main strengths	1. 2. 3.
When using my first serve, I want to . . .	1. 2. 3.
When using my second serve, I want to . . .	1. 2. 3.
When returning first serves, I want to . . .	1. 2. 3.
When returning second serves, I want to . . .	1. 2. 3.
When on the baseline, I want to . . .	1. 2. 3.
When at the net or approaching the net, I want to . . .	1. 2. 3.
When my opponent is at the net, I want to . . .	1. 2. 3.
Key drills to use	1. 2. 3.
Technical skills required	1. 2. 3.
Physical skills required	1. 2. 3.
Mental skills required	1. 2. 3.
Competition goals	

From R. Antoun, 2007, *Women's Tennis Tactics* (Champaign, IL: Human Kinetics).

Figure 6.2 Sample completed tactical profile form.

Name: A. Player Date: 1 January	Player's Signature: A. Player Coach's Signature: A. Coach
My game style	An attacking baseline player who likes to finish points at the net
Role model(s)	Maria Sharapova, Kim Clijsters, and Daniela Hantuchova
Main strengths	1. My ability to generate pace on my forehand 2. I can hit topspin and slice on the backhand side 3. I have good volley and smash technique
When using my first serve, I want to . . .	1. Dictate by using the serve and groundstroke attack tactic 2. Use my forehand as a second shot as much as possible 3. Maintain a first serve percentage of over 60 percent
When using my second serve, I want to . . .	1. Mix up the direction of my serve (especially use body serve) 2. Look to neutralise with my second shot 3. Use slice to keep the ball low
When returning first serves, I want to . . .	1. Neutralise by hitting down the middle early on in a match 2. Use my slice backhand to absorb the pace of the serve 3. Vary my returning position to break the server's rhythm
When returning second serves, I want to . . .	1. Hit as many forehand returns as possible from inside the court 2. Return and sneak when my opponent is under extreme pressure 3. Not let the server regain a neutral position in the rally
When on the baseline, I want to . . .	1. Use my inside-out forehand as much as possible 2. Maintain variety by hitting topspin and slice backhands 3. Defend using the high and low recovery shot when forced wide
When at the net or approaching the net, I want to . . .	1. Use the short angle volley after sneaking in to the net 2. Hit the smash into big targets on the court 3. Not feel that I have to hit a winning volley immediately!
When my opponent is at the net, I want to . . .	1. Make her play the volley by using the two-ball pass 2. Only use the lob when my opponent is close enough to the net 3. Pass crosscourt more often than down the line
Key drills to use	1. Basket drill: three big forehands hit from anywhere on the baseline 2. Backhand crosscourt rally: hit slice down the line and play out 3. First serve down middle and look to hit forehand as second shot
Technical skills required	1. Create space around the ball in order to hit big forehand 2. Contact point in front in order to hit effective backhand slice 3. Hit around outside edge of ball to create enough angle for volley
Physical skills required	1. Continue work on lower-body strength to help leg drive on serve 2. Quick first two steps forward needed when using sneak tactic 3. Stability needed when playing open stance recovery shots
Mental skills required	1. Maintain aggressive mentality on all first serves 2. Anticipate as many sneak opportunities as possible 3. Accept the need to defend on some second serve points!
Competition goals	Qualify for Junior Nationals and achieve a top 10 national age group ranking by the end of the year

her skills against a range of opponents. Making astute and responsible decisions throughout each match will be a major challenge, and those decisions will depend directly on the game style she brings to the court. The following sections examine decision making, problem solving, and responsibility, and the part they play in game style development.

Decision Making and Problem Solving

Tennis is such a fascinating sport because so many variables can affect the outcome of a match. Such variables come from three main sources: a player's own actions (i.e., physical factors such as technique, tactical intention, fitness levels, and psychological factors such as confidence, motivation, and concentration); her opponent's actions; and external events that affect both players (i.e., weather conditions, court surface, umpiring decisions). How a player allows these factors to influence her tactics is critical.

The key to successful tennis lies in managing all these potential influences and making the best tactical decisions regarding them as the momentum of the match ebbs and flows. In general, the most successful players manage to problem-solve and find a way to win within their own game style. In other words, they make fine adjustments rather than huge changes to their game. An example is an aggressive baseline player struggling to make an impact against a very consistent opponent. Her plan is to put pressure on her opponent by attacking from the baseline, but she makes too many errors in the process. She decides to make an adjustment to her game by trying to hit more balls out of the air as drive volleys, as well as looking to come in to the net more often to break her opponent's rhythm. By doing this, she maintains her tactical intention (attacking from the baseline), but she simply finishes the points in a different way (using drive volleys and volleys). This fine-tuning of tactics is likely to work because she is maintaining her tactical base instead of attempting to play a totally unfamiliar game. Conversely, she may decide to make a much bigger change to her tactics by trying to serve and volley or play defensively from the baseline. Such big changes are less likely to work because they are too far removed from her basic game style. They may help her alter the momentum of the match initially, but they are unlikely to prove successful for long periods of time. Small tactical adjustments often don't have to last long. Sometimes, making a slight change for only a few points is enough to change a losing game into a winning one. This is because an opponent who is only marginally ahead in a match can easily have her rhythm and confidence broken.

Many tactical decisions a player makes in a game will be based on what a player already knows about her opponent. If she has played or watched her opponent before, she will have an idea of her opponent's strengths, weaknesses, and preferred tactics. She will also have an idea as to what tactics to use against her. Scouting future opponents becomes an important part of a player's responsibility as she moves into the senior game. Indeed, scouting is a key role for many professional coaches on the WTA Tour. They analyse the patterns of play used by potential rivals and brief their player accordingly. In particular, they note how each player plays in crucial situations because this will usually indicate their most favoured tactical patterns.

Good coaches know, however, that there is a fine line between gathering information on an opponent and overanalysing how she plays. It is important for a player to know what she may expect from her opponent because this knowledge erases any fear of the unknown and helps promote feelings of control and confidence in her decision making. However, she must not allow her opponent's potential game style to dominate her own tactical intentions. In other words, a player should have a clear tactical plan going into each match with some idea of what tactics to expect from her opponent also. This could be something specific such as expecting the wide serve from the advantage court from an opponent on big points because this is her favourite serve. Or it could be something more general such as knowing that she enjoys approaching the net on short balls. This simple information helps the player prepare for the battle ahead, yet allows her to keep her focus primarily on her own game.

To hone her decision-making and problem-solving skills in all situations, a female player must experience as many open practice situations as possible. Open practice involves using drills and exercises that require her to make tactical choices, alongside playing enough realistic practice sets and matches. This differs from a closed practice, in which each player has predetermined targets to hit to without needing to make shot selections based on her tactical position (hitting only crosscourt, for example). Female players use closed practices (repetitively hitting balls without any real tactical consequence) more often than their male counterparts do. This is because, in many cases, there are simply not enough girls on a squad, or at a club, to practice with. A player who is overexposed to closed practices will lack opportunities to practice problem solving. She could easily turn into just a good 'ball hitter' without developing a well-rounded game style that helps her beat a variety of opponents. She could even lose her appetite for competition itself, or become fearful of it, because she hasn't experienced enough of it.

Coaching Tip

The coach's task is to make open practices feel as similar to match situations as possible. A realistic amount of match tension needs to be created to test the decision-making process of each player. A coach can create a matchlike situation in practice by recreating a match atmosphere. Following are some tips for creating matchlike situations in practice:

1. Make the court look like a match court. Place one chair on either side of the net for each player to sit on. Make sure that singles sticks are put in the correct place, and clear the court of any extra balls and equipment.

2. Don't allow the players to talk to each other throughout points play (unless specific feedback is required).

3. Use a scoreboard.

4. Ask an adult to umpire (preferably someone who is not closely connected to either player, such as a club member or another coach).

5. Ask the players to wear their match kit.

6. Ask the players to follow their tournament match routines (e.g., warm-up and cool-down before and after the match).

7. Open new balls at the start of a new set (budget permitting!).

8. Put a consequence on the result (i.e., 'the winner receives . . .' and 'the loser has to . . .').

Even at the highest level, female players tend to choose male practice partners because they can physically challenge them to their maximum. Indeed, the majority of coaches and practice partners on the WTA Tour are male. However, their style of play often differs greatly from that of female players (e.g., they use different spins, a different pace, and different court positions). As a result, open practice may be more unrealistic than if the female player were playing against another female player. The bottom line is that female tennis players need female practice partners, open practice, and points play to keep practice as close to match conditions as possible.

Coaches have to work hard at creating open practice situations as often as possible. The following practice drills do this by encouraging a player to make decisions and problem-solve from a variety of different playing situations. They require her to use her most favoured tactics and patterns, as well as experiment with new ones, to shape her overall game style.

- A player plays points with a spare ball in her pocket. If at any time she thinks that she has lost the point because of a poor tactical choice, she is allowed to restart the point by hitting her spare ball to a more appropriate target area. For example, if she chooses to play down the line, but realises that she should have played crosscourt, she can hit her spare ball crosscourt and finish playing the point. Her coach should make sure she can differentiate between a poor tactical choice and a poor technical execution (i.e., a player may make a good tactical choice but simply miss the shot).

• A pack of tactical playing cards is used at the beginning of every game. Each card has a different game score written on it, and some cards include a joker. This joker describes a certain tactic that the player must use for all, or part, of the game. For example, the card sets the game score at 30–0, but the joker requires the server to serve and volley on every first serve. Another card may set the game score at 15–40, but the joker requires the returner to play a drop shot within the next two points. The player tries to win the game from the predetermined score using the assigned tactics. This exercise will help her to problem-solve (i.e., figure out how to win) using tactics that may be unfamiliar to her. Indeed, she may start to use some of these tactics more if they prove successful in practice.

• When playing points, the first point of every game counts double. This simple scoring adjustment highlights the importance of winning the first point and rewards concentration and commitment to a game plan immediately. This is a key drill because it forces the player to think about her most preferred patterns of play. She will end up being dictated by her opponent if she either doesn't have a preferred pattern of play or doesn't use it straightaway. In other words, it forces her to do what she does best from the start.

• A player can win a game only by winning three points in a row. This is an important number because statistics show that a player who wins a series of three points in a row will often achieve a high success rate in tennis. This drill encourages the player to consistently play to her strengths. She will need to figure out which patterns will prove most successful against each opponent and will need to play to these almost all the time. As a result, a player's game style should be clear for all to see by the end of this practice.

• A player who reaches game point must win it at her first attempt; otherwise, her score in the game is reduced to zero. For example, the server serves at 40–15 up in her service game. If she wins the point, then she wins the game as normal. If she loses the point, then the score becomes 0–15. The server moves back to zero, and the returner remains on her previous score. (Note that there are no deuce points when using this scoring system.)

This scoring system highlights the importance of the player taking her first opportunity to win the point, and of her fully committing to her most favoured pattern of play. This is a theme that remains extremely relevant to women's tennis today because many of today's top players seem to play more bravely at vital moments during a match. Therefore, female players should practice playing these big points on a regular basis.

- Players play points from specific game scores and set scores (e.g., the server starts from 15–30 down in every service game). This gives the player the chance to practice playing from a particular situation that challenges her. Some players play well when they are behind in the score but find it hard to close out a match when in front. In this case, for example, they could play a number of practice sets starting at 4–2 30–0 up. This will immediately put them in a winning position and give them the chance to practice 'finishing the job'. The reverse score will help enhance a player's fighting spirit and will encourage her to problem-solve and find a way to win when clearly the underdog. Players can also start playing from an even score at an advanced stage in the set. For example, playing sets from 4–4 means that there can be no room for slow starters! This score puts pressure on both players to perform immediately, requiring them to impose their game styles on each other straightaway.

- When playing practice sets, players should play two more games *after* the set has finished. This is important because players often play only single sets in practice, whereas in a match they have to perform for much longer. Responding well to the loss of a set is a key mental and physical skill that needs to be practiced. A player must learn to view a new set as a new start, and she needs to make some important decisions at this time in the match. Does she need to change her tactics, or does she simply need to play better with the same game plan? The same principle applies to the player who has won the set. Does she have the ability to maintain her momentum? These two extra games allow both players to practice these skills, and are often enough to give an indication as to how the next set will unfold.

Responsibility

A player should feel the need to take more responsibility for her tennis as she matures. This means making more tactical decisions about her own game, as well as studying an opponent's game in order to problem-solve more effectively. These things will grow in importance as she progresses through the four stages of development. Encouraging a player to take responsibility and ownership of her game will significantly help her to make intelligent decisions and to problem-solve wisely as she begins to play at a senior level (stage 4). By doing this, she will continually be able to add to her game style in the most relevant way for her—with the experience of every match counting toward this. Being able to control her own tennis journey in this way will fill her with confidence and belief. Starting at an early age (or at the beginner level), the player can be expected to do the following, which will develop her sense of responsibility:

Players who take responsibility for their tennis will grow in confidence and self-belief.

- 'Publicly' state her tactical goals at the beginning of a practice session. This is a very effective way of encouraging a player to take responsibility for her own performance. In a squad session, each player can set herself a tactical target that the rest of the group can evaluate and give feedback on as the session progresses. For example, a player may tell the group that she will try to hit every second serve return from inside the baseline. Later, the group will let her know whether they believe she achieved this goal.

- Set tactical goals for her practice partner. The player should do this after playing some open points. The relevance of the goals that she sets for her partner will show how much she has learned from playing against her. This exercise encourages a player to closely note the tactical intentions of her opponent.

- Set her own targets down on the court. Examples of targets include serving targets, depth targets, and volley targets. This task will help the player feel more in control of the practice session because she is deciding where to hit to. It will also teach her to set realistic, responsible goals for herself, and to do so quickly.

- Set her own time limits for each drill. The player should decide, for example, whether each drill will last for two minutes, three minutes, or four minutes. This will give her control of her practice session by allowing her to set her own work/rest ratio. The coach can then assume more of an advisory role, giving the player more responsibility for her tennis development.

• Set her own performance level for each drill. The drill ends once the player has attained the level she set. This could be, for example, achieving a certain score in the target count drill, a certain number of serves hit into the correct target area, or a certain number of sneaks used during points play. Setting goals is crucial because players need to experience success in a drill before progressing.

• Shout 'yes!' when she believes she has executed a specific shot or tactic well enough. This gives the player the chance to play the point out during a drill if she hits two or three 'yes' shots in a row. This is an excellent way of gaining valuable performance feedback from the player. This exercise provides a number of learning opportunities for everyone. Coaches and players can discuss, for example, who agreed with the 'yes' shout, and what constitutes a 'yes' in the first place.

Summary

☐ A player's overall game style will be based on her technical ability, physical ability, and personality. Each of these factors will develop at varying times and at varying rates as the player matures. As a result, her game style must be allowed to develop over the long term.

☐ Four key stages of a female player's tennis development take into account her physical and psychological rates of growth: stage 1 (5 to 9 years old, or adult beginner), stage 2 (9 to 12 years old, or adult improver), stage 3 (12 to 16 years old, or adult club or regional player), and stage 4 (16 years old and older, or national player and above).

☐ During stage 1 a player will be developing her core movement and coordination skills, as well as having a lot of fun! Tactically, she will start by trying to simply get the ball over and in, as well as trying to move her opponent around the court and recover to a good position between shots. She will have an understanding of the game, the rules, and the meaning of competition by the end of this stage, and she will be able to play some kind of competitive match.

☐ Stage 2 represents a vital period for developing stroke technique and receiving skills. A player will be looking to build her points by using a sequence of shots and will be using more tactical variety by playing in all five game situations. This will include approaching and playing at the net and playing against an opponent who does the same. During this stage a player's own style of play is first introduced.

☐ A female player can often make rapid progress during stage 3, as she begins to compete with more senior players. By the end of this stage, her game style will be far more defined, and she will be using tactics that are very specific to her. She should be comfortable playing in all five game situations and will want to start to excel in some of them.

☐ During stage 4 a player should be looking to take complete responsibility for her game. There is a strong emphasis on smart decision making and problem solving, as well as on her ability to successfully compete on different court surfaces and in unfamiliar surroundings. She will be looking to maximise her strengths and minimise her weaknesses by using her favourite patterns of play as often as possible.

☐ Players develop patterns of play by simply combining their best shots. A player must understand where to hit the ball so that each shot builds on the previous one. Also, the serve and the return should be included in as many patterns as possible. The player needs to maximise her opportunities to use her strengths and minimise exposing her weaknesses. To develop winning patterns of play, a player needs to reflect on how she wants to play and where her strengths lie.

☐ The outcome of a tennis match can be affected by a number of variables that stem from three main sources: a player's own actions, her opponent's actions, and external events that affect both players. How a player allows these variables to influence her is critical. From a tactical perspective, the most successful players find a way to win without making big changes to their game. They either choose to fine-tune their tactics, or make no adjustments at all and simply try to play better. Scouting future opponents will help a player make more informed tactical decisions when necessary.

☐ Tactical awareness will be enhanced by using as many open practice situations as possible. This means using drills and exercises that require a player to make decisions and problem-solve as much as possible. Realistic match conditions need to be created during practice sets to fully test these decision-making skills. Also, giving a player the chance to take responsibility for her game whenever possible will be hugely beneficial to her in the long run.

GLOSSARY

absorbing slice—A groundstroke hit with slice that is used to absorb the pace of an opponent's groundstroke. It is usually played from the backhand side and can be hit to either a deep or short target.

ace—A serve in which the returner fails to return or even touch the ball. The point is won immediately by the server.

advantage—The point that is played after deuce. The player who has the advantage and wins the next point wins the game.

advantage court—The left-hand side of the court from which the server serves (i.e., left of the centre mark).

aggressive loop—A groundstroke that is hit high over the net with topspin, played with the intention of pushing the opponent deep (and often wide).

all-court player—A player who is comfortable playing from all areas of the court and who regularly finishes her points at the net.

anticipation—The ability to predict where the opponent is likely to play her next shot.

approach shot—A shot hit with the deliberate intention of coming in to the net after it is hit.

attacking shot—A shot that creates an opportunity to finish the point.

Australian formation—In doubles, when the server's partner stands at the net on the same side of the court as the server—directly in the line of the crosscourt return.

back behind—A wrong-footing shot that is hit back in the direction of a player's previous shot. It is most effectively played when an opponent anticipates a shot to the other side of the court.

backspin—A player hits the bottom of the ball to make it spin backward while it moves forward. This spin is often used with the drop shot to make the ball stop quickly.

baseline—The line at either end of the court (parallel to the net) from which the server serves.

baseline control—When a player uses her groundstrokes to control the point from the baseline. Her aim is to prevent her opponent from regaining a neutral playing position during the point.

baseline player—A player who relies on strong groundstrokes hit from the baseline to win the majority of her points.

baseline rally—A point that is played with both players hitting groundstrokes from a baseline position.

big point—A crucial point that determines which player holds an advantage in the match; for example, a break point or a set point.

block—A short, 'punched' groundstroke that is usually hit for control against a fast oncoming ball. It is often used as a return against a strong serve.

body serve—A serve that is deliberately hit in the direction of the returner's body to 'cramp' the returner's swing.

bounce smash—A smash that is hit after the player allows the ball to bounce on her side of the court.

break of serve—When the server loses the break point and therefore loses her service game.

break point—The point in a game at which the returner can break an opponent's serve (i.e., 0–40, 15–40, 30–40, and Adv-out).

building shot—A shot that creates an opportunity to attack.

centre mark—The small line across the middle of the baseline. The server must be on the correct side of this line when serving.

chip and charge—A tactic used when a player hits her sliced return of serve as an approach shot. It is a planned approach tactic often used against a second serve.

closed practice—A practice that requires a player to hit to predetermined targets without needing to make shot selections based on her tactical position. It is often used when learning, or refining, stroke technique.

contact point—The point of impact between the oncoming ball and the player's racket.

cooperative rally—A rally in which opponents work together to achieve a common goal.

counterpuncher—A player who absorbs the pace of her opponent's shot and sends the ball back with a high degree of accuracy and consistency. A counterpuncher generally prefers that her opponent attack first in the rally.

crosscourt shot—A shot played diagonally across the court from either the right or left side.

defending shot—A shot that attempts to prevent the opponent from finishing the point.

deuce—When both players in singles (or both teams in doubles) have 40 points each.

deuce court—The right-hand side of the court from which the server serves (i.e., right of the centre mark).

double bluff—A tactic used when under pressure from the baseline; a player fakes a movement across the baseline (as if to defend the other side of the court) before returning to her original position as the opponent is about to hit her shot.

double fault—A first and second serve fault in the same point. The server loses the point immediately.

double-handed—A player who keeps both hands on her racket during the shot. This is usually seen on backhand groundstrokes in particular.

down-the-line shot—A shot played straight down the court from either the right or left side.

drive-in return—A tactic used when a player hits her topspin return of serve as an approach shot. It is a planned approach tactic often used against a second serve (similar to the chip and charge).

drive volley—A volley hit using groundstroke technique that creates pace and spin on the ball.

drop shot—A shot that is deliberately hit very short over the net; it is usually played best when the opponent is positioned deep behind the baseline.

end game—The shot (or shots) that a player consistently uses to win the point.

feed out the hand—When a coach or player starts the drill with a groundstroke rather than a serve.

finish volley—A volley used to finish the point (i.e., the last shot in the rally).

first strike mentality—A player's attitude of wanting to dominate the rally before her opponent does (i.e., by getting the first significant 'strike' in first).

flat serve—A serve that is hit without any type of spin on it.

flight path—The way the oncoming ball moves. The five characteristics of flight path are direction, height, depth, speed, and spin.

floating ball—A ball that crosses high over the net without pace.

footwork—The way a player positions herself for her next shot. This could include movement to, around, or away from the ball.

forced error—When a player is pressured into making an error by her opponent.

game point—The point needed for the server to win her game (i.e., 40–0, 40–15, 40–30, and Adv-in).

games-based coaching—A method of coaching that encourages a player to play in open practice situations and develop technical skills that help her to achieve her tactical goals.

game style—A player's game style is shaped by her physical, psychological, and technical ability, and represents how she plays the game.

grand slam event—The four major tennis tournaments in the year (Australian Open, French Open, Wimbledon, and US Open).

groundstroke—A shot hit after the ball has bounced, either from the forehand or backhand side.

groundstroke attack—A tactic in which a player attacks an opponent with a strong, aggressive groundstroke as her second shot after either serving or returning.

half volley—A ball that is hit immediately after it has bounced off the ground (i.e., the player makes contact on its upward bounce).

high-percentage shot—A shot hit with a high margin of error (e.g., into a big target area).

I formation—In doubles, when the server's partner crouches at the net in the centre of the court, and the server hits the serve from directly behind her on the baseline.

inside-in forehand—When a player deliberately runs around her backhand side to hit a forehand down the line. The inside-in backhand is the opposite.

inside-out forehand—When a player deliberately runs around her backhand side to hit a forehand crosscourt. The inside-out backhand is the opposite.

instinctual approach—When a player decides to approach the net after seeing the effectiveness of her previous shot.

intercept volley—In doubles, when the partner of either the server or returner intercepts a crosscourt rally with a volley.

late return—When the returner, against a strong serve, contacts the ball 'late' (e.g., the return is hit with a contact point closer to her body than desired). This will affect the direction of the return.

lob—A shot hit high over the head of the net player either with topspin or as a 'blocked' slice. It can be used as an attacking or defending option.

margin of error—The amount of error a player allows herself for every shot. Some shots will be hit with a higher margin of error than others.

match point—A point that either player (or doubles team) needs to win the match.

midcourt ball—A ball that lands in the middle of the court.

neutral tactical position—When neither player (or doubles team) holds an advantage in the rally.

open practice—Points play or practice drills that encourage decision making and problem solving.

parallel play—In doubles, when playing partners move forward, sideways, and backward together to prevent big gaps from opening between them on the court.

passing shot—A groundstroke played when an opponent is approaching or at the net. The passing shot can be played crosscourt, down the line, or straight at the net opponent.

patterns of play—The shot sequences a player uses to execute her most favoured tactics.

perception—The ability to read the actions of an opponent and the flight path of the oncoming ball.

planned approach—When a player decides to approach the net before hitting her shot—no matter what the outcome.

receiving skills—The skills that allow a player to 'time' her shots against a variety of opponents' shots. In particular, this means being able to absorb pace, deal with different types of spins, and hit the ball while on the run.

recovery shot—A shot that is hit when a player has been forced out of position from the baseline (either deep or wide, or both). It is used as a means of recovering her tactical position in the point.

returning stance—The position on the court that a player takes up when she is about to return serve. This may differ for a first serve return compared to a second serve return.

running drives—A playing pattern that requires a baseline player to move across the baseline to hit alternate forehands and backhands, either crosscourt or down the line.

scouting—The act of watching a potential future opponent play to gain information about how she plays.

serve and volley player—A player who is most comfortable playing at the net. She often uses her serve and her return to approach the net with, and relies heavily on good volley and smash technique.

set point—A point that either player (or doubles team) needs to win the set.

short angle—A shot that is hit to a short and wide area of the court. This could be a groundstroke, volley, or smash.

shoulder-high attack—A groundstroke hit from shoulder height, usually played from inside the baseline, with the intention of applying time and pace pressure on an opponent.

single-ball feed—When a coach feeds only one ball in isolation to a player—compared to feeding consecutive balls either in a pattern or at random.

slice serve—A serve that is hit with slice. The ball 'slides' off the ground with a low bounce.

smash—A shot that is hit against a ball that travels over and above the head of the net player. It is hit using serve technique and requires precise positioning underneath the ball.

split-step—A small step with both feet (also known as a check-step or deweighting) that balances the body and allows a player to move in any direction as an opponent is about to hit the ball.

switch shot—A groundstroke hit down the line from a crosscourt rally.

the T—Where the middle line joins the service line.

time pressure—Pressure applied to an opponent by restricting the time she has to hit her next shot.

topspin serve—A serve that is hit with topspin. The ball 'kicks' off the ground with a high bounce.

two-ball pass—A tactic that requires a player to deliberately hit a high-percentage passing shot with the aim of making an opponent play a volley. Very often, the opponent doesn't hit this volley well, giving the player a chance to play a simple second passing shot or lob.

unforced error—When a player makes an error without being under any pressure from her opponent.

variety of shot—The ability to hit a range of different shots in a match.

volley—A shot that is hit before the ball is allowed to bounce.

winner—A shot that an opponent cannot reach (or barely touches with her racket).

WTA—Women's Tennis Association, also known as the WTA Tour. In 2005 the WTA changed its name to the Sony Ericsson WTA Tour.

REFERENCES

Dent, P., and P. Hagelauer. 2001. Specialty shots. In *World-class tennis technique*, ed. P. Roetert and J. Groppel, 233. Champaign, IL: Human Kinetics.

IBM, Meg Stavrakopoulou, personal communications with author, 2006.

O'Donoghue, P., and B. Ingram. 2001. A notational analysis of elite tennis strategy. *Journal of Sports Sciences* 19:107–115.

Pluim, Babette. 1999. Conditioning and medical aspects on the female tennis player. *ITF Coaches Review* 18:15–17.

US Open official Web site. 2006 Women's Singles, Finals, Match Statistics. http://www.usopen.org/en_US/scores/stats/day19/2701ms.html (accessed January 26, 2007).

INDEX

Note: The italicized *f* and *t* following page numbers refer to figures and tables, respectively.

A

absorbing slice 91
accuracy 16-17, 37, 40, 87-88
adult players, training 179-180, 181
age factors 176-177
aggressive loop 90-91, 118
aggressiveness
    in court position 76, 94-95, 122
    with drive volley 133-134
    with middle return 59
    with second serve 56-68
all-court style xviii, xix
anticipation 144-145, 160
approach. *See* planned approach
attack, from baseline 93-97
attacking forehand 28
attack position, transition from neutral 87-88
Austin, Tracy xvii-xviii
Australian formation 14, 15, 37, 49-50

B

backhand 5-6, 65
baseline
    assessing play 101-103
    attacking from 93-97
    building from 84-93
    changing direction of ball 110
    defending from 97-101
    drills 107-129
    higher tempo play 109
    running drives 111
    summary 104*f*
baseline control 7-9, 60-61, 78
baseline player, opponents at net 166-167
baseline style xvii-xviii, xix
Black, Cara 12
blocked lob 163-164
blocked return 52-54, 75
body serve 19
bounce, hitting at top of 122

breaking serve, key factor in 49
building shots 84-87, 87-88, 88-93

C

Capriati, Jennifer xviii
centre of gravity 45
chip and charge 64-65, 66
clay court, and gender xvii
Clijsters, Kim xviii, 99
coaching, games-based 178
coaching tips
    backhand slice as return 8
    bonus points for winning rally 141
    holding one service game against partner 16
    movement patterns practice 164
    open practice 190
    playing points without ball 92
    positive performance reward 86-87
    practicing with three serves per point 5
    returning practice 54
    second bounce power marker 6
    shot direction variation 88
    tactical roles during points play 100
communication 15-16, 47
consistency 84-87
control 8-9, 33. *See also* baseline control
coordination skills 177
counterpunching 18-19, 96-97, 124
court diagram 103
court position, aggressiveness in 94-95, 122
court surfaces, and gender xvi-xvii

D

Davenport, Lindsay xviii
decision making 188-192
deep angle volley 138
deep-down-the-line volley 137, 138-139, 151
deep middle approach 136
deep slice approach 142
deep volley crosscourt 138

defending
   from baseline 97-101
   with depth 125
   with double bluff 165-167
   drills for 125-129, 159, 173
   against drop shot 100-101
defensive skills 97-98
Dementieva, Elena 97
Dent, Paul 86
diamond drill 116
direction 17-19, 40, 42
dominance 2-16, 29, 41, 77
double bluff, defending with 165-167, 173
double-handed returner 17-18
doubles team
   baseline defence 100
   defending as 128
   intercept volley 156
   at net 157, 174
   net defence 159
   one-up/one-back position 141-143
   opponents approaching net 166-167
   playing from baseline 95
   return and planned approach 82
   standing ground at net 144
down-the-line approach 136-137
drills
   about xx
   baseline play 107-129
   net play 148-160
   opposing net player 170-174
   tactical returning 72-82
   tactical serving 28-42
drive-in tactic 66
drive volley
   after return 79
   attack with 148
   and first serve 9-10, 34
   in net play 133-134
   return and drive volley 62-63
   as server's second shot 10
drop shot 91-93, 100-101, 119, 129

E
errors, counting 85-86
Evert, Chris xvii-xviii

F
first serve
   and baseline control 7-9
   dominating with 2-16, 29
   drills for 28, 31, 32
   and drive volley 9-10, 34

and groundstroke attack 3-5
   maintaining control after 33
   neutralising first serve return 45-56
   and sneak 10, 35
   and volley 11-16
flow charts 102-103
forbidden square drill 117
forehand options, right-handed server
      4-5

G
games-based coaching 178
game styles xvii-xviii, 176
gender differences xv-xvii, 94, 132, 140
ghosting. *See* sneak
Graf, Steffi xviii
grass court, and gender xvii
groundstroke attack 3-5, 57-60, 91

H
height xv, 140
Henin-Hardenne, Justine xix, 3, 21, 65,
      85, 89
high recovery shot 98-99
Hingis, Martina xix, 85, 97

I
I formation 14, 37, 48
Ingram, Billy 45
inside-in return 50-52, 74
inside-out return 48-50, 73
instinctual approach xvi, 132
instinctual net play 133-135
intercept, by server's partner 23
intercept volley 142, 156

J
junior players, training 178

K
King, Billie Jean xviii, 64-65

L
Larkham, Brent 7
left-handed return 56
left-handed serve 23-24, 54-55
lob
   aggressive and defensive 171
   against opponent at net 163-165
   over server's partner 53-54
   as return to approach net 67-68
   and running pass shot 172
lower-body strength xv
low recovery shot 98-99

M

Maes, Carl 115
match flow charts 102-103
maturity, and gender xvii, 89, 180-181
Mauresmo, Amelie xix, 3, 11, 65
men, female players compared to xv-xvii, 94, 132, 140
mental skills 182
middle return 46-48, 59, 72
Molik, Alicia 21
movement efficiency 164
movement skills 177
Myskina, Anastasia 85, 97

N

Navratilova, Martina xviii, 12, 64-65
net, dominating as serving team 37
net errors, counting 85-86
net play
about 132
anticipation 144-145
assessing 167
doubles team at net 157, 159
instinctual approach 133-135
opponent approaching net 162-167
planned net play 135-143
standing ground 143-144, 158
summary 168f
neutral position 60, 87-88

O

O'Donoghue, Peter 45
one-up/one-back position 141-143
open practice 189-192
opponent
approaching net 162-167
getting clues from 44
returning habits of 23
scouting future opponents 189
studying movement and stroke 145

P

pace 20, 46
partner
anticipation by 13
communication with 15-16
intercept by server's partner 23
tactical goals for 193
patterns of play xix-xx, 184-185
percentages
points won at net, serving and returning 132t
recording baseline play in 103

returns 68
serves 24-25
winning shots 84-85
perception skills 95, 120
performance level, for drills 193-194
personal factors 185, 188-194
personality development 181
planned approach
about xvi, 132
doubles return and planned approach 82
in net play 135-137
return and planned approach 64-68, 81
shot development 150
planned net play 135-143
point statistics, second serve 56, 57t
position, aggressiveness in 94-95, 122
posture 44
power, variety of 42
problem solving 188-192

Q

quality shots, counting 107

R

rally, average length of 45
rally target 85
Raymond, Lisa 12
reaction 44
reading ball 44
ready position 44
reception skills 177
recovery shot 98-100
responsibility 192-194
returning percentages 68
returning summary 69f
return of serve
from aggressive court position 76
aggressive second serve return 56-68
anticipating direction of 4
blocked return 52-54
doubles return and planned approach 82
inside-in return 50-52, 74
inside-out return 48-50, 73
left-handed return 56
against left-handed serve 54-55
maintaining baseline control 78
middle return 46-48
neutralising first serve return 45-56
pressure on returner 54
return and baseline control 60-61

return of serve *(continued)*
   return and drive volley 62-63
   return and groundstroke attack 57-60
   return and planned approach 64-68,
      81
   return and sneak 63-64, 80
   tactics 44-45
   women's reliance on xvi
rhythm 20, 46, 60
right-handed server, forehand options 4-5
running drives, from baseline 111
running pass shot and lob 172

S
Sabatini, Gabriella xviii
Sanchez-Vicario, Arantxa xvii-xviii
Schnyder, Patty 24, 97
second serve
   accuracy of 16-17, 37
   aggressive second serve return 56-68
   disguising direction of 40
   dominance by moving returner out of
      position 41
   dominance with second serve return 77
   left-handed servers 23-24
   making effective 16-24
   neutralising point with second serve
      pattern 39
   pace and rhythm 20
   pattern visualising returner's court
      position 38
   point statistics 56, 57t
   spin 21-23
   variety of direction 17-19
Seles, Monica xvii-xviii
serve
   dominating first serve 2-16
   effective second serve 16-24
   first serve and baseline control 7-9
   first serve and drive volley 9-10
   first serve and groundstroke attack 3-5
   first serve and sneak 10
   first serve and volley 11-16
   holding when opponent knows tactic
      30
   men's reliance on xvi
   tactics 2
   varying direction and players'
      movements 22
   against weak net player 7
serve and volley tactic
   about 11-16
   blocked return against 53
   middle return against 47
   practicing 36
   as preferred style xviii
   return against 67
serving percentages 24-25
serving speeds 2
serving summary 25f
shadow-swinging practice 92
Sharapova, Maria xviii, 3, 17, 85
short angle 89-90
short angle approach 135-136
short angle topspin 142
short angle volley 137-139, 151, 165
shot quality 93
shot variety tactic xix
shoulder-high attack 95-96, 123
side, weaker *vs.* stronger on second serve
      17-19
slice
   absorbing slice 91
   returning left-handed slice serve 54-55
   short angle slice 90
   slice approach 135-136, 142
   slice return 66-67
   slice second serve 22
smash
   defending against 165
   in net play 140-143
   power and direction 152
   volley combined with 154, 155
   winning with 153
sneak
   after return 80
   and first serve 10, 35
   with inside-out return 49
   return and sneak 63-64
   sneak volley in net play 134-135
sneak volley 149
space, not pace drill 119
speed, of serve 2
spin 21-23, 42. *See also* topspin
stable base 45
stance 46
standing ground at net 143-144, 158
Stosur, Sam 21
switching, down the line 87
switch shot, defending against 126

T
tactical anticipation 160
tactical awareness xviii-xx, 91
tactical development
   about 176-177

beginner level 177-179
club/regional level 180-182
improver level 179-180
national/international level 182-184
tactical goals, stating 193
tactical profile form 186-187f
target hits, counting 114-115
targets, setting own 193
technical anticipation 160
Tiley, Craig 88
time limits, for drills 193
topspin
short angle topspin 90
topspin lob 163
topspin return 66
topspin second serves 21
touch and feel 93
two-ball defence 127
two-ball pass 162-163, 170

U

unforced errors 85, 108
upper-body strength xv, 140

V

variety, in building shots 88-93
volley
defending against 165
and first serve 11-16
at net 137-139
smash combined with 154, 155

W

warm-up errors, counting 85
weaknesses, minimising 177, 184-185
whipped topspin short angle
groundstroke 136
Williams, Serena xviii, 9
Williams, Venus xviii, 9
winning patterns of play 184-185
winning shots percentages 84-85
women, male players compared to xv-
xvii, 94, 132, 140

Y

'yes' shots 194
young players, training 178

ABOUT THE AUTHOR

Rob Antoun is manager of the junior performance programme at Sutton Tennis Academy, an international training center located in London. In this role, he works with both players and their coaches on tennis tactics, technique, physical conditioning, mental skills, and tournament programming. A former ATP world-ranked tennis player, Antoun has coached 45 international senior and junior tennis players over a 16-year period, including two top-ranked senior British players, Lucy Ahl (2001) and Lizzie Jelfs (1996). From 1996 to 2001, he coached Hannah Collin, a British junior who reached a top 15 junior world ranking and played Federation Cup for Britain. Antoun also served as a national coach for the British Lawn Tennis Association (LTA) from 1994 to 2002, coaching five Federation Cup players and numerous British senior and junior national champions. Antoun is a PCA-qualified coach and is one of a select group of LTA-endorsed coach education tutors. He is also joint founder and codirector of Pro Tennis Solutions, a company that provides a wide range of coaching education services in tennis. He also holds a degree in psychology. Antoun resides in Kent, England, with his wife, Catherine, and son, Jake.

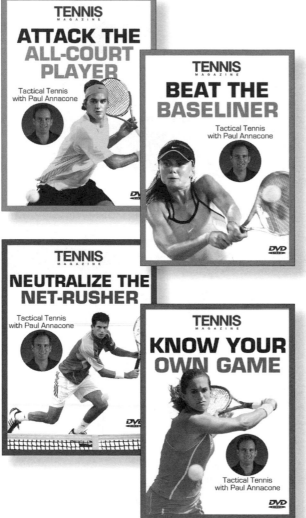